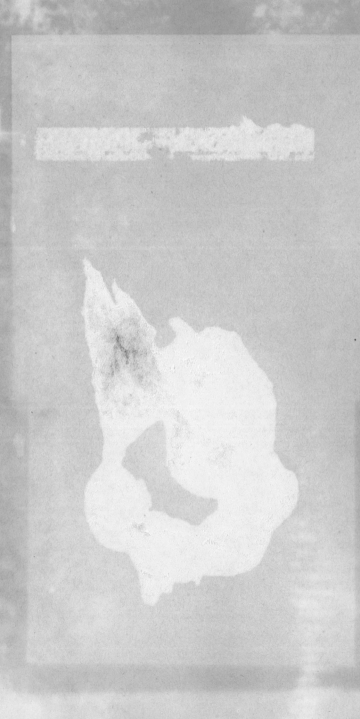

THE NEW FORGET-ME-NOT

A CALENDAR

THE
NEW FORGET-ME-NOT

PRESENTED TO:

....

BY:

....

THE NEW FORGET-ME-NOT

A CALENDAR

Contributors

ANON.

SIR GEORGE ARTHUR

MAURICE BARING

MAX BEERBOHM

CLIVE BELL

HILAIRE BELLOC

LORD BERNERS

EDMUND BLUNDEN

IVOR BROWN

GODFREY CHILDE

CYRIL CONNOLLY

BERNARD DARWIN

RICHARD ELWES

TYRONE GUTHRIE

IAN HAY

FATHER RONALD KNOX

SHANE LESLIE

ROBERT LYND

ROSE MACAULAY

DENIS MACKAIL

Decorated
by
REX WHISTLER

MCMXXIX

Contributors

RAYMOND MORTIMER

HAROLD NICOLSON

NAOMI ROYDE-SMITH

ELIZABETH RYAN

E. SACKVILLE-WEST

V. SACKVILLE-WEST

SIEGFRIED SASSOON

CHRISTOPHER SCAIFE

EDWARD SHANKS

J. C. SQUIRE

CHRISTOPHER SYKES

LORD THOMSON

H. M. TOMLINSON

PHILIP TOMLINSON

THE MARQUIS OF
TWEEDDALE

JOHN VAN DRUTEN

HUGH WALPOLE

GEORGE WANSBROUGH

DOROTHY WELLESLEY

R. H. WILENSKI

COBDEN-SANDERSON

1 MONTAGUE STREET

LONDON

Printed in Great Britain for
R. COBDEN-SANDERSON, LTD.
by WALTER LEWIS, M.A., *at*
the Cambridge University Press

ERRATA

Page 27. The number of oars appearing in the illustration should be 8, not 16.

Page 31. Gentlemen taking part in the Grand National do not, as is here depicted, wear top hats on their heads. Jockey caps, suitably strengthened in order to minimize the risks of concussion, are *de rigueur*.

Page 49. It is necessary for all ladies who are present at one of Their Majesties' Courts to wear three feathers and a veil. It is not confined, as in the drawing, to *débutantes*.

INTRODUCTION

IN the shadowy past, just before the iron railway and the submarine cable, the revolving Year was celebrated by our innocent-looking ancestors with pretty pocket-books, known as the Annuals. Between 1820 and 1840 these talismans multiplied. Scarcely a publisher failed to cultivate an Annual. The winter blossomed with Keepsakes, and Amaranths, and Bijoux, and Souvenirs; appealing petals of sentiment were scattered in the path of the season, and Marianas in moated granges smiled correctly over the newest poems and pictures.

Among those Annuals, Mr Ackermann's Forget-Me-Not was eminently eligible. On its presentation-scroll Aunt Selina wrote her stiffest Italian hand; the not unmindful young Araminta preserved the yearly gift in the original freshness suggested by that name Forget-Me-Not. Thinking of these tinted niceties (without which, "what is a day, what is a year?"), we have been at some pains to produce for our times this New Forget-Me-Not. The times are more hurried, sentiment is less freely confessed—we grant such variations. Our almanack is intended to answer modern feelings, and—here we have varied the Forget-me-Not constitution—by providing a daily *register, we have accepted the new pace of our old friend the Year. Long may he flourish, with all the usual attractions, from his first clear chimes to his last doleful knell! We come to praise and not to bury him, to protect his days and salute his festivals in our* New Forget-Me-Not.

The publishers desire to express their good fortune in the number of illustrious persons who have adorned the scythe and hourglass with their verse and prose; they also venture to congratulate themselves, and the public, on the pictures, dust-wrapper and binding design by Mr Rex Whistler, whose wit, fancy, humanity and technique would make Mr Ackermann agreeably envious, and the fine old steel-engravers " sigh, and look, and sigh again."

CONTENTS

WINTER

SUMMER

AUTUMN

COLOURED PLATES

CALENDAR : 1930

JANUARY	FEBRUARY	MARCH	APRIL
S . 5 12 19 26 ..	S . 2 9 16 23 ..	S . 2 9 16 23 30	S . 6 13 20 27 ..
M . 6 13 20 27 ..	M . 3 10 17 24 ..	M . 3 10 17 24 31	M . 7 14 21 28 ..
Tu . 7 14 21 28 ..	Tu . 4 11 18 25 ..	Tu . 4 11 18 25 ..	Tu 1 8 15 22 29 ..
W 1 8 15 22 29 ..	W . 5 12 19 26 ..	W . 5 12 19 26 ..	W 2 9 16 23 30 ..
Th 2 9 16 23 30 ..	Th . 6 13 20 27 ..	Th . 6 13 20 27 ..	Th 3 10 17 24 .. ..
F 3 10 17 24 31 ..	F . 7 14 21 28 ..	F . 7 14 21 28 ..	F 4 11 18 25 .. ..
S 4 11 18 25	S 1 8 15 22	S 1 8 15 22 29 ..	S 5 12 19 26 .. ..

MAY	JUNE	JULY	AUGUST
S . 4 11 18 25 ..	S 1 8 15 22 29 ..	S . 6 13 20 27 ..	S . 3 10 17 24 31
M . 5 12 19 26 ..	M 2 9 16 23 30 ..	M . 7 14 21 28 ..	M . 4 11 18 25 ..
Tu . 6 13 20 27 ..	Tu 3 10 17 24	Tu 1 8 15 22 29 ..	Tu . 5 12 19 26 ..
W . 7 14 21 28 ..	W 4 11 18 25	W 2 9 16 23 30 ..	W . 6 13 20 27 ..
Th 1 8 15 22 29 ..	Th 5 12 19 26	Th 3 10 17 24 31 ..	Th . 7 14 21 28 ..
F 2 9 16 23 30 ..	F 6 13 20 27	F 4 11 18 25	F 1 8 15 22 29 ..
S 3 10 17 24 31 ..	S 7 14 21 28	S 5 12 19 26	S 2 9 16 23 30 ..

SEPTEMBER	OCTOBER	NOVEMBER	DECEMBER
S . 7 14 21 28 ..	S . 5 12 19 26 ..	S . 2 9 16 23 30	S . 7 14 21 28 ..
M 1 8 15 22 29 ..	M . 6 13 20 27 ..	M . 3 10 17 24 ..	M 1 8 15 22 29 ..
Tu 2 9 16 23 30 ..	Tu . 7 14 21 28 ..	Tu . 4 11 18 25 ..	Tu 2 9 16 23 30 ..
W 3 10 17 24	W 1 8 15 22 29 ..	W . 5 12 19 26 ..	W 3 10 17 24 31 ..
Th 4 11 18 25	Th 2 9 16 23 30 ..	Th . 6 13 20 27 ..	Th 4 11 18 25 .. ..
F 5 12 19 26	F 3 10 17 24 31 ..	F . 7 14 21 28 ..	F 5 12 19 26 .. ..
S 6 13 20 27	S 4 11 18 25	S 1 8 15 22 29 ..	S 6 13 20 27 .. ..

1931

JANUARY	FEBRUARY	MARCH	APRIL
S . 4 11 18 25 ..	S 1 8 15 22	S 1 8 15 22 29 ..	S . 5 12 19 26 ..
M . 5 12 19 26 ..	M 2 9 16 23	M 2 9 16 23 30 ..	M . 6 13 20 27 ..
Tu . 6 13 20 27 ..	Tu 3 10 17 24	Tu 3 10 17 24 31 ..	Tu . 7 14 21 28 ..
W . 7 14 21 28 ..	W 4 11 18 25	W 4 11 18 25	W 1 8 15 22 29 ..
Th 1 8 15 22 29 ..	Th 5 12 19 26	Th 5 12 19 26	Th 2 9 16 23 30 ..
F 2 9 16 23 30 ..	F 6 13 20 27	F 6 13 20 27	F 3 10 17 24 .. ..
S 3 10 17 24 31 ..	S 7 14 21 28	S 7 14 21 28	S 4 11 18 25 .. ..

MAY	JUNE	JULY	AUGUST
S . 3 10 17 24 31	S . 7 14 21 28 ..	S . 5 12 19 26 ..	S . 2 9 16 23 30
M . 4 11 18 25 ..	M 1 8 15 22 29 ..	M . 6 13 20 27 ..	M . 3 10 17 24 31
Tu . 5 12 19 26 ..	Tu 2 9 16 23 30 ..	Tu . 7 14 21 28 ..	Tu . 4 11 18 25 ..
W . 6 13 20 27 ..	W 3 10 17 24	W 1 8 15 22 29 ..	W . 5 12 19 26 ..
Th . 7 14 21 28 ..	Th 4 11 18 25	Th 2 9 16 23 30 ..	Th . 6 13 20 27 ..
F 1 8 15 22 29 ..	F 5 12 19 26	F 3 10 17 24 31 ..	F . 7 14 21 28 ..
S 2 9 16 23 30 ..	S 6 13 20 27	S 4 11 18 25	S 1 8 15 22 29 ..

SEPTEMBER	OCTOBER	NOVEMBER	DECEMBER
S . 6 13 20 27 ..	S . 4 11 18 25 ..	S 1 8 15 22 29 ..	S . 6 13 20 27 ..
M . 7 14 21 28 ..	M . 5 12 19 26 ..	M 2 9 16 23 30 ..	M . 7 14 21 28 ..
Tu 1 8 15 22 29 ..	Tu . 6 13 20 27 ..	Tu 3 10 17 24	Tu 1 8 15 22 29 ..
W 2 9 16 23 30 ..	W . 7 14 21 28 ..	W 4 11 18 25	W 2 9 16 23 30 ..
Th 3 10 17 24	Th 1 8 15 22 29 ..	Th 5 12 19 26	Th 3 10 17 24 31 ..
F 4 11 18 25	F 2 9 16 23 30 ..	F 6 13 20 27	F 4 11 18 25 .. ..
S 5 12 19 26	S 3 10 17 24 31 ..	S 7 14 21 28	S 5 12 19 26 .. ..

I KNOW (I do not affect ignorance) that the Cinema is of two kinds; the one I am told dying, the other, I am assured, being born. But I have heard that of other things such as Spain and Australia; Theocritus and the *Daily Express*; the Creed and Dirt. The dying was called The Movies, an American word; the borning is, I am quite sure, called The Talkies—surely also an American word? Of the last kind I have seen none—I mean, heard none. Therefore I am well equipped for judging them.

Indeed, in this matter let me tell you the story of the Fox-Hunting Undergraduate of Balliol and the Embryo Bishop of that same College. I heard it with my own poor ears—which is more than I can say of The Talkies. The E.B. said to the F.H.U. "What do you think of Kant?" The F.H.U. said, "I think he's all rot." The E.B. said with a sneer, "May I ask whether you have ever read Kant?" The F.H.U. answered genially, "Not a word!" "Then," said the E.B. angrily, "how can you judge him?"

"By the people who reverence him," said the F.H.U. genially again, thereby scoring several points, a bull's eye, a knock-out, honours, a goal to nothing, six love, 256 not out, and three below the line. Also Check Mate.

Of Movies (to return to these) I have seen three good ones: really, thoroughly good. I then saw about two dozen bad ones, after which I gave it all up. I have seen (1) *The Three Masks*, (2) An admirable Italian film, (3) A thing about animals; and the only reason I do not say, "Oh, Lord, now dismiss thy Servant in peace" is that I think the word "Servant" far too high sounding. If I were not afraid of being prosecuted for blasphemy I should delete the word "servant" and the word "thy" and substitute the words "this poor devil." I forget, by the way, whether the ritual phrase is "delete" or "omit"—but it doesn't matter.

When I am dead there will arise a man called Hannibal J. Growpy (or some such name). He will have a great deal of money. It will occur to him that what people want to see in this new and detestable art is one of four things: (*a*) fun, (*b*) miracles, (*c*) things they have already seen, (*d*) the past. Hannibal will exploit this idea (having a lot of capital) and will become even more rich than he is—I mean, than he will be, for he is yet but a puling child.

There will be no more sob-stuff, there will be no more Sheriffs, there will be no more Cowboys, there will be no more Love-flop or Close-ups or Aged Mothers—in a word, there will be no more Gutter Stuff.

And God will wipe away all tears.

At any rate, I hope so.

2

MEMORANDA

WEDNESDAY 1*st*

THURSDAY 2*nd*   THURSDAY 1*st*

FRIDAY 3*rd*   FRIDAY 2*nd*

SATURDAY 4*th*   SATURDAY 3*rd*

𝔖𝔲𝔫𝔡𝔞𝔶 5*th*   𝔖𝔲𝔫𝔡𝔞𝔶 4*th*

MONDAY 6*th*   MONDAY 5*th*

TUESDAY 7*th*   TUESDAY 6*th*

WEDNESDAY 8*th*   WEDNESDAY 7*th*

THURSDAY 9*th*   THURSDAY 8*th*

FRIDAY 10*th*   FRIDAY 9*th*

SATURDAY 11*th*   SATURDAY 10*th*

Sunday 12*th*   Sunday 11*th*

[4]

THE CONTINENTAL BOAT TRAIN

ROSE MACAULAY

THE people of Great Britain have always a passionate
    desire to travel by a boat train;
    Partly because they believe that in the places to which
such a train will convey them there will be less rain,
But chiefly because Britons who stay long in one country
    have always got bored,
So from the earliest centuries onwards they have gone in for
    paying visits abroad.
Regard us now, as we board the train at Victoria for one
    of those sea-side towns beyond which Britain ceases;
Mark with what eagerness we rummage in pockets, ruck-
    sacks and valises,
Hoping that the indispensable objects left behind
Do not include our passports, those ultimate imbecilities of
    the lost idiot official mind.
Observe our furtive concentration as we open little phrase
    books and brood
Over remarks so essential to international intercourse as
    "*Get me a better portion. Don't give me the outside cut. This*

5

*is overdone, underdone, too fat, too lean, take it away. Of
course the portions can be divided? Now bring us an entrée,
it does not matter what, provided that it is good.*"

Oh marvellous continental meals! Oh course following
course of succulent foreign fare!

Maccaroni, tortillas, wienerschnitzel, poulet and haricots
verts!

Oh plump little Gauls, oh beautiful Latins, oh touching
and bun-fed Teutons! Oh poplars, oh cafés on pave-
ments, oh futbal in plazas, oh ravishing, noisy Nea-
politan nights!

Oh snows of Andorra and scorched Andalusian cities and
Switzerland's shocking heights!

Wild and bright are our dreams of you as we sit tight and
reserved in our tight reserved places—

Lunn's tourists, family parties, young men and maidens with
ruck-sacks, large ladies with eau-de-cologne and mother-
sill in dressing-cases,

Cool and cosmopolitan bachelors and spinsters with travelled
and worldly faces.

Lo, mark how, on sighting the ocean, these are transformed
into a wild and sea-faring horde

Who leap from the train and run, each striving desperately
to arrive first abroad.

(And they hope, oh they hope, fond romantics, that in no
pension, albergo, fonda, café, piazza, casino, tramvia,
Biergarten, musée, Alp, or Haute Pyrénée will they
have the misfortune to encounter again

Any one of those mild British faces which they have viewed
with such natural distaste for two hours on the Continental Boat Train.)

6

MONDAY 13*th*   MONDAY 12*th*

TUESDAY 14*th*   TUESDAY 13*th*

WEDNESDAY 15*th*   WEDNESDAY 14*th*

THURSDAY 16*th*   THURSDAY 15*th*

FRIDAY 17*th*   FRIDAY 16*th*

SATURDAY 18*th*   SATURDAY 17*th*

Sunday 19*th*   Sunday 18*th*

MONDAY 20*th*   MONDAY 19*th*

TUESDAY 21*st*   TUESDAY 20*th*

WEDNESDAY 22*nd*   WEDNESDAY 21*st*

THURSDAY 23*rd*   THURSDAY 22*nd*

FRIDAY 24*th*   FRIDAY 23*rd*

SATURDAY 25*th*   SATURDAY 24*th*

𝔖𝔲𝔫𝔡𝔞𝔭 26*th*   𝔖𝔲𝔫𝔡𝔞𝔭 25*th*

CONCERTS   EDWARD SACKVILLE-WEST

Beware of the person who says he never goes to concerts because the people, the hall, etc., prevent him from enjoying the music: he is first cousin to the numerous family of those who "have no time for reading"; the truth being that music bores him—though he dares not say so.

There are better reasons than this for not going to concerts, one of them being that—in England at any rate—they are always at least half an hour too long: on the Continent they do not often err in this way. A more serious objection is the unwritten law according to which programmes are almost invariably chosen, e.g. the overture to *Poet and Peasant* (to prove to those of the audience who are already seated and glaring at those who are shuffling over their feet, that the orchestra—though not yet by any means all there —is by now a little less outside the hall than before), the chief soprano aria from *Der Freischütz*, a short tone poem called *Saklatvala*, or some such name, the *Second Symphony*

9

of Brahms, and finally *Pomp and Circumstance* or the Ballet Music from *Faust*.

If, instead of making programmes on the principle of the London Coliseum, conductors would select (say) three works, whose collocation in one programme had some organic justification and would altogether last not more than one and a half hours, orchestral concerts would be more often worth going to than they are at present.

The objection to soloists is the same; they are in fact even more depressing because, however bad an orchestra may be, it is seldom as intolerable as a bad soloist—and nearly all soloists are bad, even when they call their concerts "Special Scriabine Recital", where the word "special" has no function except that of concealing mediocrity.

In the eighteenth century, concerts were apt to last all day; but the audience did not think of listening all the time. They talked, flirted, went away and came back. Nowadays it is possible for us to adopt the same admirable plan, by turning off the wireless, or—with the added advantage that we can select the programme ourselves—on the gramophone.

MONDAY 27*th*   MONDAY 26*th*

TUESDAY 28*th*   TUESDAY 27*th*

WEDNESDAY 29*th*   WEDNESDAY 28*th*

THURSDAY 30*th*   THURSDAY 29*th*

FRIDAY 31*st*   FRIDAY 30*th*

SATURDAY 31*st*

MEMORANDA

SATURDAY 1*st*

𝖘𝖚𝖓𝖉𝖆𝖞 2*nd*   𝖘𝖚𝖓𝖉𝖆𝖞 1*st*

CRUFT'S   PHILIP TOMLINSON

IN the days when it still was possible to reach our mother's skirts we were towed to Cruft's to see lap-dogs. But it was the big fellows who wrung from us loud sounds of ecstasy and moved in our hearts the vices of acquisition; our inconsequential minds to-day recall the lap-dog, who went unheeded then, only to wonder where now his diminutive lordship seeks repose. That abbreviated fashions have not ended his thin-spun life, but merely made anomalous his name, there is the evidence in 1930 as in that first show in 1886, when the indomitable Mr Cruft started the Derby of Dogdom. The aristocrats have their own displays. Here puppies and novices are tried out, old champions meet all comers, grandsires are beaten by grandsons. All stout-hearted breeders will maintain that their secret comes by no acquired skill but is inborn, like the secret of all the great arts, to be perfected by long practice and deep meditation. Calm amid the joyous, challenging, hysterical babel, serious figures bend over exhibits which might be treasures, heirlooms, old masters, with hands on knees, heads slowly nodding in mysterious appraisement. These are the artists. They speak in the dialects of all the counties. In crowd-thronged rings dogs parade under the watchful eyes of the judges: languid, graceful Borzois; Bedlingtons caricaturing the gentle lamb; bulldogs who have never met a bull; wolf-hounds who should pray they never meet a wolf, for the papers chronicle the death of one from fright when a mongrel but bristled at him; sheep dogs who have never guarded sheep; spit dogs who have never turned a spit; ever popular terriers whose muzzles grow steadily longer; pugs who grow more noseless in the procession of the years; and, best of all, the dogs that are bred for the love of the breed, dogs of our childish exultations: the Newfoundland; the wall-eyed bob-tail who herded his charges through the market town; Old English collies; plum pudding dogs who ran behind the doctor's gig; sad-faced bloodhounds; gay little Yorkshires. Here are aliens newly introduced: gazelle-eyed Afghans and lion dogs. Some still faithful adherents to breeds that fashion is deserting show the Dandie Dinmont, the mid-Victorian Maltese. And as you pass along aisles of benches adorned with cards, blue, red and white, you may regret a beautiful breed lost for ever, or give a thought to old Mick, who never went with his pals to Cruft's, but whose memory is brightest in the wayside dust of life. His mother was a terrier of sorts and his father was a nightmare. He would have swept the show.

MONDAY 3rd   MONDAY 2nd

TUESDAY 4th   TUESDAY 3rd

WEDNESDAY 5th   WEDNESDAY 4th

THURSDAY 6th   THURSDAY 5th

FRIDAY 7th   FRIDAY 6th

SATURDAY 8th   SATURDAY 7th

Sunday 9th   Sunday 8th

MONDAY 10*th*   MONDAY 9*th*

TUESDAY 11*th*   TUESDAY 10*th*

WEDNESDAY 12*th*   WEDNESDAY 11*th*

THURSDAY 13*th*   THURSDAY 12*th*

FRIDAY 14*th*   FRIDAY 13*th*

SATURDAY 15*th*   SATURDAY 14*th*

Sunday 16*th*   Sunday 15*th*

ST VALENTINE'S DAY   MAURICE BARING

THE cult of St Valentine, and the observance of St Valentine's Day was the last survival of an older England, older than the England of Punch and Judy and the Muffin-man; older than the England of the Stage coach.

The England of Shakespeare, of faery Mab and the drudging goblin, who earned his cream for threshing the corn, when the whole year from the hour when the Christmas Brand was kindled and quenched on Candlemas Day, until the day when the Christmas Log was brought with a noise to the firing, was punctuated by festivals; when not only the feast days of the Saints were kept with dance and song, but there was a sequence and procession of household and rural ceremonies, such as St Distaff's Day.

> Partly work and partly play
> Ye must on St Distaff's day.

St Valentine's Day was one of the chimes that told the march of the seasons. It is perhaps a survival of something older still, for in Pagan days boys drew the names of girls in honour of the Goddess *February*. The feast of St Valentine is said to mark the day when the birds begin to mate. Charles Lamb sang its praises, for in his day, and later, until the end of the 'eighties, you bought on St Valentine's Eve your stock of Valentines. They lay in white cardboard boxes, aromatic with a particular scent; they were soft to the touch and pleasant to the eye; their appeal was sentimental; they were fringed with paper lace, and they mostly bore the picture of a Cupid aiming an arrow at a heart, and a little piece of verse.

Now all that is over. St Valentine has been banished from the new Prayer Book. There are no Valentines in the shop windows in February. But last St Valentine's Day I picked up these verses in a London street:

> The fog has hid the February skies,
> The streets are dark, and all the world is grey;
> But in the mocking sunshine of your eyes,
> Saint Valentine is keeping holiday.

Which proved that someone had sent to someone a Valentine.

MONDAY 17*th*   MONDAY 16*th*

TUESDAY 18*th*   TUESDAY 17*th*

WEDNESDAY 19*th*   WEDNESDAY 18*th*

THURSDAY 20*th*   THURSDAY 19*th*

FRIDAY 21*st*   FRIDAY 20*th*

SATURDAY 22*nd*   SATURDAY 21*st*

Sunday 23*rd*   Sunday 22*nd*

FIRST NIGHTS   IVOR BROWN

Y<small>OU</small> can hardly get in. You have come to be a
spectator of a play and a thousand spectators are
looking at you. The crowd nudges and giggles and
shoves. Who are you? Surely a Somebody! Ivor Novello
or Radclyffe Hall? Here comes Hannen Swaffer. The
Woman Who Knows swoons with frenzy. "Look!" she says,
"Forbes-Robertson!"

Inside, once more. The critics are nodding wearily to each
other like clerks coming into the office at 9 a.m. The in-
curable first-nighters have turned out, the Jewesses, like
slugs, plump and shiny, the shrewd, solid men from the
ticket-agencies, those mutes and mourners of a myriad
plays. These are the real priests of Dionysos. Will Dionysos
"do a deal" through his servants? He will not.

On it goes. The author's friends smile anxiously and clap.
No joke too awful for their loyal, devoted laughter. At home
they would just stare coldly at a man who talked such stuff.
Here it is all too wonderful. Programme girls cluster by the
back of the Circle at the ends of the Acts and clap, clap,

clap. Fools! The people who have paid for their seats are getting restive. They hate this meaningless applause.

The end. A tumult of cheering comes from the friends of the family. Silence in Pit and Gallery. "Author, Author!" roar the friends. Hide yourself, fool, thinks the critic who knows the way of these affairs. On flounders author, unpainted on the painted stage, a frail and fishlike object. He grins and starts inaudible wamblings.

The gallery can bear it no longer. There is a moan. It is the voice of the people, a wind of truth more swift but not more cold than next day's "notices". The author vanishes. So, in a few days, does the play.

Comes a new syndicate, new author, new play. Or is it same syndicate, same author, same play? Anyhow it is a First Night. You can hardly get in.

MONDAY 24*th*   MONDAY 23*rd*

TUESDAY 25*th*   TUESDAY 24*th*

WEDNESDAY 26*th*   WEDNESDAY 25*th*

THURSDAY 27*th*   THURSDAY 26*th*

FRIDAY 28*th*   FRIDAY 27*th*

SATURDAY 28*th*

MADAME TUSSAUD'S　　　　　DOROTHY WELLESLEY

TUSSAUD in flames! Policeman guard the way,
Lord sit upon your throne, 'tis Judgement Day.
Determine at this bursting of the grave,
Whom to consign to fire and whom to save.

First down the stair, Lord, see Barabbas grin,
Defeating Thee again. Now comes his kin:
"Make way for murderers!" the people shout.
"Let the saints burn—these we can do without."

Down the great stair, slung over each man's back,
A great doll leers: safe Gladstone! But alack
Victoria herself—O dreadful dream—
Forgets herself in melting into Cream;
And Oscar Wilde at last has found release
For ever in the lovely arms of Peace;
Drips Shelley's blood, his heart is burning so,
He goes headlong, the way he likes to go;
Heads without bodies fall, alas the fard,
Du Barry's gaunt, and Lamballe's run to lard;

Wellington's weak as wax and grows obese;
Great Caesar runs: excellent candles these;
Fast burns the Show upon the rising gale,
That grease spot once was Florence Nightingale.
Runs, runs the wax, and in the holocaust
Concaves are won, convexities are lost:
Women like men, and men like women grow,
What sex are these? O Lord, O dost thou know?
Shakespeare's a bubble now, and Bacon's fat,
They fall to candle grease, and stink at that.

Lord tell the dolls if fire for sin atones!
No ears are left, nor brains, not even bones.

By nineteen thirty, no by twenty seven,
Robbers and murderers are safe in heaven.

MEMORANDA

SATURDAY 1*st*

𝔖𝔲𝔫𝔡𝔞𝔶 2*nd*   𝔖𝔲𝔫𝔡𝔞𝔶 1*st*

MONDAY 3rd   MONDAY 2nd

TUESDAY 4th   TUESDAY 3rd

WEDNESDAY 5th   WEDNESDAY 4th

THURSDAY 6th   THURSDAY 5th

FRIDAY 7th   FRIDAY 6th

SATURDAY 8th   SATURDAY 7th

Sunday 9th   Sunday 8th

THE BOAT RACE   FATHER RONALD KNOX

THE Oxford and Cambridge Boat Race has been rowed between Putney and Mortlake since the year 1856. But the recent researches of Dr Hoschbein have shown that we have to go very much further back to trace the origins of the institution, which has in fact nothing to do with Oxford or Cambridge, and was not originally a boat-race at all. (Indeed, it can be shown that as late as 1829 Oxford rowed against Cambridge at Henley.)

Hoschbein was the first to see that the whole ceremony has a religious significance, and belongs to the very earliest strata of human thought. It is well known that in early times a bridge could not be built without some human sacrifice to propitiate the river god. (Cf. the *argei*, straw figures which were thrown over a bridge at Rome, and the old folk-ballad, "London Bridge is broken down", *passim*.) It is probable that the Danes, who encamped at Fulham during their invasions, introduced and localised this rite on the Thames: Hammer-smith is obviously a cultus-title of the god Thor; and its old name, Hermodswode, equally shows

27

traces of Scandinavian influence. Over Hammersmith Bridge, then, in the time of the Danish invasions, it will have been customary to throw human sacrifices; young men in the prime of life would be demanded for the purpose by liturgical considerations. The purpose of the ceremony was, of course, to secure good weather for the crops; the savage naturally assumes that rivers control the weather by sympathetic magic. And it is impossible not to feel the ingenuity of Hoschbein's suggestion that half the victims were dressed in light blue, half in dark, to represent the appearance of the sky in sunshine and in storm respectively; in all probability omens were taken by seeing which of the two contingents drowned first.

As time went on, and manners became more civilised, it is easy to see how a humanitarian instinct provided boats or coracles to save the victims from death. Their escape, however, had to be contrived as rapidly as possible, so that for ceremonial purposes they could rank as validly drowned. They would make their escape either in the direction of Putney (by derivation almost certainly Pont-Neuf, the New Bridge), or towards Mortlake (the Pool of the Dead). Hoschbein tried to prove that originally the two crews rowed in opposite directions; but Seligman has shown that this view rests on insufficient evidence. At what date Londoners relinquished their old cultus-festival into the hands of the Universities is not certain.

While it cannot be said that all the above conclusions are fully established, it cannot be doubted that they are in harmony with much that is most characteristic in modern anthropological speculation.

MONDAY 10*th*   MONDAY 9*th*

TUESDAY 11*th*   TUESDAY 10*th*

WEDNESDAY 12*th*   WEDNESDAY 11*th*

THURSDAY 13*th*   THURSDAY 12*th*

FRIDAY 14*th*   FRIDAY 13*th*

SATURDAY 15*th*   SATURDAY 14*th*

Sunday 16*th*   Sunday 15*th*

MONDAY 17*th*   MONDAY 16*th*

TUESDAY 18*th*   TUESDAY 17*th*

WEDNESDAY 19*th*   WEDNESDAY 18*th*

THURSDAY 20*th*   THURSDAY 19*th*

FRIDAY 21*st*   FRIDAY 20*th*

SATURDAY 22*nd*   SATURDAY 21*st*

Sunday 23*rd*   Sunday 22*nd*

THE GRAND NATIONAL — ROBERT LYND

THE Grand National is the most terrifying race in the world. It is also the most beautiful. The ordinary spectator sees few of the terrors, for the most dangerous jumps—the bank at Becher's Brook, from which there is a drop of six feet, and Valentine's Brook, a few score yards beyond this, with its comparable perils—are in a stretch of the oval course farthest from the stands. These are obstacles such as horses leap in legends. Walk round the course before the race, and you will find yourself marvelling that men and horses of a post-legendary age should be able to endure the test of the four-and-a-half miles race twice round the course, with its thirty jumps over piled-up fence and water.

The pains and pleasures of apprehension chase each other through one's veins from the moment at which, at the shout, "They're off!" the confused mass of horses sets off at a gallop towards the first fence and leaps over it in swift dark waves that seem almost certain to collide. Do not be surprised to hear the cry: "The favourite's down!" Another fence and another wave of horses rising to it, and more cries of speculation as to which horses have fallen. But no rider may yet have been poured over his horse's head, and there may still be a full field when horses and men disappear into the half-mist towards Becher's Brook.

Then all is imagination till the dim shapes reappear, sometimes with a riderless horse galloping side by side with the leading survivor in the race, and taking every jump alongside of him, graceful and terror-stricken, flying neck-and-neck with him across the fifteen-foot water-jump at the stands. Unseated jockeys come waddling back across the grass. The surviving horses pass, having made the first round of the course, and it is fortunate if they are half the number that started, as they gallop off for the second half of the journey.

Thin often as a defeated army is the small company of lion-hearted horses that sweep back into sight after Becher's Brook and Valentine's Brook have for the second time done their worst. Somebody shouts, "Worldwinner's leading!" But at that moment Worldwinner's heart fails him, and he lollops along like a tired cart-horse. Another horse sweeps past him with the power of a storm, and another, challenging him, seems to lead him and fall behind him at alternate springs. They reach the last fence and pass over it neck by neck. Then comes a battle for speed along the level grass, when the muscles of the spectators are almost as tense with the sense of the struggle as the muscles of the horses and their desperate riders. The horse of one's desire has now his head in front, now half his body. But not yet is the race secure. Yes, yes. He's clear. There is a triumphant yell of a longed-for name from the crowd. One's horse has passed the winning-post. The heart soars like a bird released from captivity. How beautiful the world is!

At least, so it was when Music Hall won the Grand National.

MONDAY 24*th*   MONDAY 23*rd*

TUESDAY 25*th*   TUESDAY 24*th*

WEDNESDAY 26*th*   WEDNESDAY 25*th*

THURSDAY 27*th*   THURSDAY 26*th*

FRIDAY 28*th*   FRIDAY 27*th*

SATURDAY 29*th*   SATURDAY 28*th*

Sunday 30*th*   Sunday 29*th*

MONDAY 31*st*   MONDAY 30*th*

TUESDAY 31*st*

MEMORANDA

THE COUNTRYSIDE   V. SACKVILLE-WEST

EASTER and Pentecost enclose the spring
    Like toll-gates on the turnpike of the seasons;
    Easter has set the hinges on to swing
And opened April with her lovely treasons.
Now what will April in her wallet bring
To toss along the road for our diversion?
What handfuls thrown in air of fluttering
White petals that drift down in slow dispersion?
What flock of rooks and starlings on the wing
About the heavens blown like cindered paper?
What whirl of clouds, what grasses in a ring?
What tails that frisk, what kids and lambs that caper?
April and May their generous handfuls fling
Across the meadows and along the hedges,
And artless man each year stands marvelling
At the renewal of his privileges;
Forgets each year,—poor winter's starveling,—

The spring's surprise, that faster comes and faster,
The change between each dawn and evening
Once he has passed the turnpike gate of Easter.
Then is the winter a forgotten thing,
Then is the road one swift and fair procession,
While nature holds in annual junketing
The paschal and the pentecostal session.

TUESDAY 1*st*

WEDNESDAY 2*nd*   WEDNESDAY 1*st*

THURSDAY 3*rd*   THURSDAY 2*nd*

FRIDAY 4*th*   FRIDAY 3*rd*

SATURDAY 5*th*   SATURDAY 4*th*

Sunday 6*th*   Sunday 5*th*

MONDAY 7*th*   MONDAY 6*th*

TUESDAY 8*th*   TUESDAY 7*th*

WEDNESDAY 9*th*   WEDNESDAY 8*th*

THURSDAY 10*th*   THURSDAY 9*th*

FRIDAY 11*th*   FRIDAY 10*th*

SATURDAY 12*th*   SATURDAY 11*th*

𝖲𝗎𝗇𝖽𝖺𝗒 13*th*   𝖲𝗎𝗇𝖽𝖺𝗒 12*th*

COVENT GARDEN   CLIVE BELL

IT does credit to our civilisation, the opera-house in Covent
Garden; so do Oxford and Cambridge, Lord's, Lock's,
Lord Balfour: for the moment I can think of nothing
else that does. It is the only opera-house—grand opera-
house—I have ever been in that it was a pleasure to be
in. And it is an opera-house. The others are mere business
premises, and the fact that they are utterly unsuited to the
business does nothing to mitigate their banality. But Covent
Garden is a commonwealth; box, stalls and gallery are here
les trois états. Also it is in the best English tradition that our
opera-house should keep up its dignity amidst the butt-ends
of cabbages and broccoli.

The gold and crimson of Covent Garden are the perfect
setting for our upper middle-classes; nowhere else are white
shirts and shoulders framed to such advantage. Covent
Garden is Renoir. Covent Garden is Victorian: no
eighteenth-century ghosts, no Longhis, no Lancrets, such
as haunt the Fenice or the Residenz Theater, haunt the

39

house which, nevertheless, was founded by Rich. Neither is any musical ghost to be found, no, not an echo of Handel, nor yet of

the Toso,
So very majestic and tall,
Miss Ayton whose singing was so-so
And Pasta divinest of all;

only the pleased and self-complaisant wraiths of beauties, swells and celebrities, of Lord Dundreary and Mrs Ponsonby de Tomkins. Covent Garden is the mausoleum of British society at its richest, mondaine not musical. Some day the salle Pleyel may be haunted by the spirits of a musical élite and become the monument of a phase of twentieth-century sensibility; but those who went to Covent Garden went to the opera.

Only behind the crowd of prosperous phantoms are just discernible some of a different birth, whispy, pathetic, dissolute—the ghosts of those wintry, would-be revellers, the fancy-dress dancers. As the heavy curtain falls and the still Renoirs, bunches of subscribers charmed to bouquets, dissolve in their gilt frames to become animated Degas shouldering opera-cloaks, I catch beneath the impasto an outline of poor Bessy Belwood, in tights, with the Jubilee Plunger, and some Pink'un bloods and blondes, and Phil May drunk, disguised as a Quornite.

But of a summer's evening you may still see the subscribers going to the opera in Covent Garden.

MONDAY 14*th*   MONDAY 13*th*

TUESDAY 15*th*   TUESDAY 14*th*

WEDNESDAY 16*th*   WEDNESDAY 15*th*

THURSDAY 17*th*   THURSDAY 16*th*

FRIDAY 18*th*   FRIDAY 17*th*

SATURDAY 19*th*   SATURDAY 18*th*

Sunday 20*th*   Sunday 19*th*

MONDAY 21*st*   MONDAY 20*th*

TUESDAY 22*nd*   TUESDAY 21*st*

WEDNESDAY 23*rd*   WEDNESDAY 22*nd*

THURSDAY 24*th*   THURSDAY 23*rd*

FRIDAY 25*th*   FRIDAY 24*th*

SATURDAY 26*th*   SATURDAY 25*th*

𝔖𝔲𝔫𝔡𝔞𝔶 27*th*   𝔖𝔲𝔫𝔡𝔞𝔶 26*th*

PUNTING   MAX BEERBOHM

Very evocative, yes, this little picture; particularly so,
poignantly so, to one who has beheld with the eyes of
boyhood the very things Rex Whistler has but recon-
structed from hearsay and from documents. *Tout passe,
tout casse, tout lasse.* "Changing London." *Hélas!* The March
of Time. *Vixere fortes. Eheu fugaces.* All, all are gone, the old
familiar faces. *Et ego in Arcadia.*

Very Arcadian, yes, Hyde Park still was when the Ser-
pentine flowed up within a few feet of the Marble Arch,
reflecting on its way the sallow and rounded northern houses
of Park Lane—the house that was once Mrs Fitzherbert's,
and all those others. I cannot say that I much liked the
Quadriga that had been put upon the Arch to commemorate
the Shah of Persia's visit in 1873. It was (I still think) one
of Boehm's least good works. But I was rather furious when
it was removed by a short Act of Parliament in 1881. And
I was mad with rage when, some nine years later, I saw
demolished the dear old moss-grown Rockery, a structure of
uncertain origin, but redolent of the mermaid who had from

43

time immemorial, and till so recently, swum around and about it.

While she lived, one had taken her as a matter of course. She was just one of the normal anomalies of our town, like the two milkmaids in St James's Park, or the Piccadilly goat; and, like them, she was very decorous—except on the one occasion which Rex Whistler has recorded. Heaven only knows what she saw in Mr Spingham. She cannot have liked his blazer or his pince-nez or his black kid gloves. I knew him and Mrs Spingham slightly (*very* slightly, I am glad to say) and am the man whom you see in the distance bowing to them from a hansom at the moment of the mermaid's sudden rising from the water. I heard Mrs Spingham's scream; I saw her loss of balance, her immersion, and her gallant rescue by the mermaid. I supposed she would be grateful, be forgiving. But she was hardly dry before she began writing violent letters to the Press. Questions were asked in the House of Commons. The Ranger of Parks bowed under the storm, and by his order the mermaid was shot. I shall always maintain that this was murder.

MONDAY 28*th*　　　　　　MONDAY 27*th*

TUESDAY 29*th*　　　　　　TUESDAY 28*th*

WEDNESDAY 30*th*　　　　　WEDNESDAY 29*th*

THURSDAY 30*th*

MEMORANDA

MEMORANDA

THURSDAY 1*st*

FRIDAY 2*nd*   FRIDAY 1*st*

SATURDAY 3*rd*   SATURDAY 2*nd*

𝔖𝔲𝔫𝔡𝔞𝔶 4*th*   𝔖𝔲𝔫𝔡𝔞𝔶 3*rd*

THE PRIVATE VIEW   R. H. WILENSKI

CARS. Huge, glittering, sleek cars. Clusters of chauffeurs. Photographers. Police.

Rambler roses and sickly hydrangeas (a limp and thirsty guard of honour) lining the stairs.

Backs. Backs moving upward. Sleek backs, backs of beauties, backs of old ladies, backs of bishops, backs of belted earls. Backs, too, of the wrong people who have somehow secured tickets.

Turquoise blue catalogues handed with a bow by attendants in scarlet robes. Turquoise and scarlet—the Garter ribbon, the General's tunic—the Academy's pet chord.

Faces. Faces in frames. Faces on the move. Famous faces. Plain and coloured faces. Near faces—much too near.

Artists (Burlington House Brand—Refuse All Substitutes). Johnnie Walker stocks and ivory canes. (Still going strong. Pictures Guaranteed the Same.) Women painters in sombreros. Dustmen exhibitors in costume. Prodigies in prams.

"We got back last Thursday—But, my dear, how perfectly divine—Fancy hanging that, it's only half finished—They found she had a tumour—Don't forget to mark the catalogue —What's the name of the fellow who paints trees?—I've lost a stone in eighteen days—Where is the rejected picture? —That stands out well, one can almost touch it—She looks much older off the stage—I'm here for one of the papers —So am I, my dear—How screaming, so am I—and I—and I—and I...."

Oil paintings. Seven hundred. "Autumn Leaves", "Margaret, daughter of Brig.-Gen. Sir Blank Twoshoes", "Interior at Twoshoes Hall", "A-hunting we will go", "Sunset on the Dee", "The Blue Bead", "The Coral Necklace", "The Jade Ring"....

Watercolours. Three hundred. "Old Houses at Rye", "February", "March", "April", "Le Clocher", "Cuckoo"....

Miniatures. One hundred. "Joyce", "Marjorie", "Ethel", "Polly", "Annette", "Susette", "Carina", "Jenny in Grandmother's Best Gown"....

Marbles and Bronzes. Two hundred and fifty. "A Dryad", "A Faun", "Pipe on!" "Leda", "Bellona", "James Brown, Esq.", "John Jones, Esq.", "Jack Smith, Esq.", "The Late Josephus ('Jimmie') Robinson, Esq.", "The Wounded Flea"....

Architecture. No time for that....

One o'clock. Down the stairs. Through the portals. The photographers' chance. Click, click, click. The sleek car. The slammed door. Puff, puff, puff. How these chauffeurs over-oil.

48

THE COURTS   NAOMI ROYDE-SMITH

Fragments from Canto V of an unpublished work entitled
"Miranda's Year"

THOUGH finished in her manners and her mind,
Ascot[1] and Paris both now left behind,
Miranda of perfection still falls short:
She's not yet made her curtsey at a Court

.   .   .   .

.   .   .   . it dawns in May,
The much prepared-for, liberating day.

For this Miranda and the Bosom-Friend[2]
Have laboured: "*One, Two, Three*, advance and bend
Four—with the left foot—*Five, Six*, taking pains
At *Four* to kick away your clinging trains":
For this the haughty dress-maker has laid
Wonders of satin, treasures of brocade
In yards on chairs and along th'expensive floor
Where dames compete and *débutantes* adore:

[1] The girl's Eton.   [2] Vide Canto IV.

For this the ostrich-feather merchants vie
Each claiming that he can, alone, supply
Plumes that at once are opulent and neat;
While every jeweller in Grafton Street
Displays a clasp for shingled heads, designed
To keep the things erect, secure, *behind*.[1]

.　　.　　.　　.　　.　　.　　.

And, long before the sunset's level rays
Have set the sky above the Mall ablaze
Eastward from Barnes, westward from Finsbury Square
Typist and clerk and landlady repair
To stand, and wait, and stare, and stare, and stare.

In Bond Street studios see the steady light
Of Court photographers throughout the night.
The incessant lift shoots up and shivers down
With Ladies Jones and Robinson and Brown
Eager to see, next day, their names and dress
Recorded by the illustrated Press.

.　　.　　.　　.　　.　　.　　.
.　　.　　.　　.　　.　　.　　.

Now, from the Palace windows light has died
And the last footman leaves the chauffeur's side.[2]
Homeward to Bayswater and Kensington
Miranda's last admiring friend has gone;
And she herself, unveiled, un-trained, at last
The long, long wait, the short Encounter past,
Feels, for a moment, sad, because the splendid,
Royal, important, tiring day is ended.

[1] "H.M. the Queen has expressed a wish that feathers be worn erect at the back of the head and not drooping to one side as it was remarked had been the case in several instances at the Courts last year." *Daily Press.*

[2] "Ladies attending the Courts are informed that a footman must accompany each car arriving at and leaving the Palace." *Ibid.*

MONDAY 5*th*   MONDAY 4*th*

TUESDAY 6*th*   TUESDAY 5*th*

WEDNESDAY 7*th*   WEDNESDAY 6*th*

THURSDAY 8*th*   THURSDAY 7*th*

FRIDAY 9*th*   FRIDAY 8*th*

SATURDAY 10*th*   SATURDAY 9*th*

Sunday 11*th*   Sunday 10*th*

MONDAY 12*th*   MONDAY 11*th*

TUESDAY 13*th*   TUESDAY 12*th*

WEDNESDAY 14*th*   WEDNESDAY 13*th*

THURSDAY 15*th*   THURSDAY 14*th*

FRIDAY 16*th*   FRIDAY 15*th*

SATURDAY 17*th*   SATURDAY 16*th*

𝔖𝔲𝔫𝔡𝔞𝔶 18*th*   𝔖𝔲𝔫𝔡𝔞𝔶 17*th*

THE FLOWER SHOW DENIS MACKAIL

THERE comes a time of year when suddenly I can no longer take my dogs in the garden behind Chelsea Hospital, for mammoth marquees are rising all over it, rocks and topiary are arriving in large lorries, and there is no more admission except on business. Then I realise that another summer is here, and that the greatest of all Flower Shows is returning to welcome it. What masses and banks of colour will blaze under those canvas roofs in a day or two from now, what experts will assemble from the ends of the earth, what cunning gardeners from big country-houses, what quantities of rich nature-lovers vying with each other in the exchange of long Latin names. How ignorant I shall feel as I am caught up in the vast crowds and sucked this way and that. And again there will be that little stab of emotion when in a quiet backwater I find the red-coated pensioners selling their home-made pincushions.

But is this what I think of when I hear the magic words, "Flower Show"? No, I am in the heart of the country, in July or August, in a field where two or three weatherbeaten tents are stocked with the floral and vegetable pride of the neighbourhood. But these are not what have brought me here. The smell of crushed grass, of gunpowder and hot engine-oil, the sound of a steam organ and the crack of miniature rifles, such, I am afraid, are what give me that special thrill, however gigantic the pumpkins or hideous the assorted jars from the cottagers' gardens. How delicious it is when the dew begins to fall, and the flares come out on the stalls, and the village band thumps and tootles in the distance. The glory of Chelsea seems extraordinarily remote, but for some reason my own youth seems extraordinarily near.

MONDAY 19*th*   MONDAY 18*th*

TUESDAY 20*th*   TUESDAY 19*th*

WEDNESDAY 21*st*   WEDNESDAY 20*th*

THURSDAY 22*nd*   THURSDAY 21*st*

FRIDAY 23*rd*   FRIDAY 22*nd*

SATURDAY 24*th*   SATURDAY 23*rd*

Sunday 25*th*   Sunday 24*th*

THE FOREIGN OFFICE   HAROLD NICOLSON
PARTY

In the indulgent but now distant reign of King Edward VII the Foreign Office Party was a thing indeed. The summer sun would rise above St James's Park to the sound of workmen hammering striped awnings in Downing Street, hammering awnings on the Horse Guards' Parade. ·By breakfast time the corridors of the Foreign Office would echo to a thousand diverse foot-steps —the careful slouch of those who carried mahogany, the easier shuffling of those who bore only a roll of scarlet carpeting, the embarrassed footsteps of men reeling under palms and hydrangeas, the brisk-heeled tock of the young lady from Gunters'.

As the afternoon passed a feeling of awe descended on the building; feet fell muffled on scarlet pile; the door of the lavatory was banked with azaleas; on the upper landing were rows and rows of saucers waiting for their cups.

The staff of the Foreign Office in full diplomatic uniform would assemble early, somewhat self-conscious as to their white silken legs, somewhat arrogant above their stiff gold collars, smelling of camphor and of that dab of benzine with which, at the last moment, their valets had cleaned their gloves.

The wife of the Secretary of State for Foreign Affairs, if he had a wife, would take her stand upon the half-landing, prepared, under her tiara, to smile upon a thousand faces.

To the opening bars of *Rigoletto* the guests would arrive, the women bearing on their indignant breasts such meagre baubles as diamonds and rubies, the men, supreme at last, decked with the silks and enamels of the Dannebrog, the St Olaf, the Imtiaz, the Lady of the Conception, the Alexander Newsky, the Shefakat, the White Elephant, the Golden Fleece, the Royal Victorian Chain.

Again the band would play *Rigoletto*. Processions would move from supper room to supper room: the champagne-cup would be reduced at last to a small slice of banana floating in watery dregs: and at midnight Big Ben would look down upon the Columbian Minister clasping an umbrella with an oxydised silver handle, searching for his motor in Parliament Square. One by one the great chandeliers would leap into darkness, and with a satisfied grunt the pelicans in the sedge below would settle down to sleep.

I write, however, of past glories. To-day, when there is a Foreign Office Party, people are merely asked to tea.

MONDAY 26*th*   MONDAY 25*th*

TUESDAY 27*th*   TUESDAY 26*th*

WEDNESDAY 28*th*   WEDNESDAY 27*th*

THURSDAY 29*th*   THURSDAY 28*th*

FRIDAY 30*th*   FRIDAY 29*th*

SATURDAY 31*st*   SATURDAY 30*th*

                                𝕾𝖚𝖓𝖉𝖆𝖞 31*st*

MEMORANDA

𝔖unday 1st

THE FOURTH OF JUNE · SHANE LESLIE

To all Etonians Paradise will be a perpetuation of the Fourth of June. On George the Third's birthday the old boys return and feel young while the youngest boys fancy they were never so grown up before. There is no Early School on the Fourth of June. Boys arise and array themselves in coloured raiment such as they wear on no other day of the year. The whole school makes itself radiant; those, who can, struggle into tails and bright waistcoats and high collars, while the members of the Boats don fancy dress—straw hats with flowers, white ducks and patent shoes. Coxes wear the dress of Admirals, swords and cocked hats.

In the morning the Sixth Form deliver the time-honoured Speeches in Upper School to their admiring parents and tutors. Not merely do they exhibit high standards in the vernacular, but they are often eloquent in French and perform some light mumming in Greek. The Muses having been satisfied, the rest of the day is devoted to athletics. A Gala cricket match draws crowds to the Playing Fields and the sound of the gentle summer revelry of bat and the band breaks through the heavy foliage of the elms. Absence is solemnly read by the Head Master in the School Yard from the steps of Chapel. The gushing crowd of relations and friends flock to the river and watch the Boats embark and row upstream. By the time the crews have dined and returned, it is dark and Fellows Eyot is blazing with fireworks. Star-shells, floating lights and reeling rockets emblazon the night air. The crews are expected to rise and stand to the salute as they float past. The old wine-red buildings glow in the unnatural light and a far-shot rocket brings glimpses of the distant Castle. *Floreat Etona* blazes out into letters of fire and every Etonian, old or young, retires to bed a better Etonian than before, if that is possible.

While Windsor stands, Eton will endure. While the river flows, Etonians will row and the Captain of the Boats will wield his sovereignty side by side with the Throne. While there is a Gregorian Calendar, there will be a Fourth of June.

MONDAY 2nd   MONDAY 1st

TUESDAY 3rd   TUESDAY 2nd

WEDNESDAY 4th   WEDNESDAY 3rd

THURSDAY 5th   THURSDAY 4th

FRIDAY 6th   FRIDAY 5th

SATURDAY 7th   SATURDAY 6th

Sunday 8th   Sunday 7th

THE DERBY   IAN HAY

T HE British nation goes to the Derby, as it goes to
war or to bed, because at the moment there seems to
be no possibility of anybody doing anything else. In
other words, no Englishman likes to feel out of the movement
on Derby Day.

That is why the man who has never seen a race-course in
his life, who has not the remotest idea what "Six to Four the
Field" means, and who quite frequently believes that the
Derby is run at Derby, suddenly feels it incumbent upon
him, for about a week at this time of the year, to take an
interest in the Turf. With a jovial, Derby-comes-but-once-
a-year expression, he buys from his stenographer a ticket in
the office sweep. He spends Derby Day, as usual, at his
office, in an agony of apprehension, until, about ten minutes
past three, the result of the race is shouted in the streets. Then
he heaves a deep sigh, tears up his ticket, and becomes a
perfectly normal citizen for another fifty-one weeks.

But in addition to the millions of Englishmen who celebrate the Derby in the manner I have just described, there are a certain number who actually go there. How many, you will not realize until you find yourself jammed in the bottle-neck of Ewell High Street, with a balloon-decked charabanc in front of you and a highly vocal motor-bus behind, and a zealous but utterly untimely gentleman bearing a banner which promises that The Wicked Shall Be Turned Into Hell on your flank.

All the world goes to the Derby. The Services, Politics, Society, Art, Literature, the Stage, Big Business—you will see their chosen leaders in high places everywhere, in boxes, or on the tops of coaches, or walking about like everyone else. You will see, too, scores of Dominion and American visitors, who simply dare not go home and confess that they spent a summer in England and never went to the Derby. And everywhere, boisterous or reserved, exultant or wistful, according to their mood and disposition, you may observe our returned exiles—brown-faced Englishmen from India, or Singapore, or Kenya, or Trinidad, from all the continents or islands where the Flag flies—home once more for a brief spell, to feast their eyes upon (to us) such ordinary spectacles as a green English field or a London policeman. These are the men who value the Derby at its right worth. Ascot is well enough; it is London, and London is all right. But the Derby is—"this blessed plot, this earth, this realm, this England!".

MONDAY 9*th*   MONDAY 8*th*

TUESDAY 10*th*   TUESDAY 9*th*

WEDNESDAY 11*th*   WEDNESDAY 10*th*

THURSDAY 12*th*   THURSDAY 11*th*

FRIDAY 13*th*   FRIDAY 12*th*

SATURDAY 14*th*   SATURDAY 13*th*

Sunday 15*th*   Sunday 14*th*

THE TROOPING OF THE COLOUR

SIR GEORGE ARTHUR

A FOREIGNER of distinction has declared that the Eton and Harrow match, the Royal Tournament, and the Trooping of the Colour are the three occasions which would be burnt indelibly into his memory, not only on account of their merits but because they are incapable of imitation, or of reproduction anywhere else than in England.

The growth of the relations between the Birthday Parade and the "illuminated and highly coloured version of the daily mounting of the King's Guard"—is just now under expert examination, and some points of interest are likely to be forthcoming, but the ceremony has been such a fruitful theme for the chronicler that a word might not be amiss as to some of the personnel who figured in it.

During the long period when the Duke of Cambridge held the post of Commander-in-Chief, it fell to him—in the Sovereign's accustomed absence—to take the salute at the Trooping of the Colour. But when, in 1895, Lord Wolseley succeeded to the supreme post, he raised a very natural objection to his predecessor holding the Parade if to himself were assigned a subordinate position. Queen Victoria promptly solved the difficulty by giving instructions that the Prince of Wales should thenceforward represent her and take the salute. In this century the Sovereign, until last year, has always been present at every Birthday Parade, and although Army Councillors and Military Attachés and other great personages were in the great cortège, King George's absence necessitated the absence of the Gold Stick whose duties are only about the person of the Sovereign and who according to appointment "always waits immediately next to the Sovereign in person before all others."

"The office of the Colonel is very honourable and a place of great consequence in the Army; wherefore he ought to be an experienced souldier, religious, wise and valiant." So runs a 17th century definition, and no better description could have been given of Colonel Brand of the Coldstream Guards who was in charge of the Parade in 1929. The Ensign—the central figure of the day—is so called from his bearing the ensign, and he was often styled "the ancient" from the French *enseigne*. The Sergeant (*serviens*), like the Roman centurion, comports himself like "a man under authority" though "having soldiers under him"; the Corporal (Italian *caporale*) recognises himself as a leader, however small the section he sways, and the great dictionary defines the soldier as "a man of military skill and experience." No wonder with such as these, blended with the superb squadron of Household Cavalry, with the Drum-Majors of the Guards in their State uniform stiff with gold, with massed bands playing as perhaps only the Guards' bands can play, there is presented year by year a pageant which grips the imagination, and sometimes chokes the throat of the spectator no less than it dazzles his eye.

MONDAY 16*th*   MONDAY 15*th*

TUESDAY 17*th*   TUESDAY 16*th*

WEDNESDAY 18*th*   WEDNESDAY 17*th*

THURSDAY 19*th*   THURSDAY 18*th*

FRIDAY 20*th*   FRIDAY 19*th*

SATURDAY 21*st*   SATURDAY 20*th*

𝔖𝔲𝔫𝔡𝔞𝔶 22*nd*   𝔖𝔲𝔫𝔡𝔞𝔶 21*st*

ASCOT   ANON.

IT is called Royal Ascot. The best of the proletariat goes
as a matter of course. It enjoys seeing what human, as
well as equine, thoroughbreds can do.

The best horses also go to Ascot as a matter of course. So
do the best caterers and the most comfortable trains. It
seems a little hard that exception to the inevitability of thus
going to Ascot should sometimes occur to the best people.

Judge well the Briton whose social standing entitles him
to alphabetical space in social registers, yet who says:
"Ascot? I hate it. I never go". Discounting the few
misogynists who go nowhere on principle, the British man or
woman who *can* attend a royal function by royal invitation
will do so, finding pleasure in pride.

The crowd that throngs the Royal Enclosure is not just
a crowd. It is a selected portion of the community that has
submitted such credentials of moral and social irreproach-
ability as have been approved by the censor of the Sovereign's
visiting list. It is a matter of national pride to realise, each

year, the growing hundreds who have sound moral and social standing in a supposedly reprobate world.

Ascot is the Walhalla of the successful. The right mothers take daughters, the right fathers pay expenses, which are high. The right sportsmen enter horses. The right horses win. Sound book-makers evince more interest in the spectacle than in book-making. Sound backers hardly bet. The most expensive clothes justify their creation, the prettiest women do likewise and have the best time. And the tallest men who belong to the best clubs come into their own in the scramble for food.

Once inside the Enclosure, Brown, Jones or Robinson can feel as proud as Duke or Marquis of his name. For every Enclosure ticket has been inscribed (within the confines of Buckingham Palace?) in copper-plate hand: "Royal Enclosure. To be worn in a conspicuous position".

Could one wear it otherwise? Would one? Certainly not!

MONDAY 23*rd*   MONDAY 22*nd*

TUESDAY 24*th*   TUESDAY 23*rd*

WEDNESDAY 25*th*   WEDNESDAY 24*th*

THURSDAY 26*th*   THURSDAY 25*th*

FRIDAY 27*th*   FRIDAY 26*th*

SATURDAY 28*th*   SATURDAY 27*th*

Sunday 29*th*   Sunday 28*th*

MONDAY 30*th*   MONDAY 29*th*

TUESDAY 30*th*

MEMORANDA

WIMBLEDON   ELIZABETH RYAN

EVERYONE knows that Wimbledon is the Mecca of
lawn tennis. It is nice to win championships in
France and America but nothing really matters in
the tennis world but a victory on the famous Centre Court.
It is the "be all" and (unfortunately for many) the "end
all" of our hopes.

Since the war the great championships have become
almost as important a social function to Londoners as Ascot
or any of the other big fixtures of the season, and year after
year the crowds of enthusiastic spectators increase. How
different is the Wimbledon scene of to-day when compared
to the original ground and buildings which were used over
fifty years ago!

What an attraction the women players have become! It
is amusing to think that they were excluded for seven years
at the start, during which time the men had it all their own
way. A championship nowadays without events for women
would be a dull affair. How different they look to their pre-
decessors who had to play under such trying dictates of

fashion—long skirts, tight waists, collars, sleeves and even hats. The 1929 stars have every comfort and freedom in the way of dress to help them and they have certainly benefited by it. Even now ideas seem to be rapidly changing and developing, so may the future look after itself!

Mlle Lenglen did more to revolutionize women's tennis than anyone. She appeared the first year after the war and astonished the world by her wonderful play as well as her grace. She stimulated popular interest in the game to such an extent that a bigger Wimbledon had to be built!

Since then all the countries have encouraged their players, both men and women, to reach the highest standard of play —so that the Wimbledon of to-day is not only a social function but a yearly rendezvous of the world's greatest players coming to compete for the world's greatest honours.

TUESDAY 1*st*

WEDNESDAY 2*nd*   WEDNESDAY 1*st*

THURSDAY 3*rd*   THURSDAY 2*nd*

FRIDAY 4*th*   FRIDAY 3*rd*

SATURDAY 5*th*   SATURDAY 4*th*

Sunday 6*th*   Sunday 5*th*

MONDAY 7*th*   MONDAY 6*th*

TUESDAY 8*th*   TUESDAY 7*th*

WEDNESDAY 9*th*   WEDNESDAY 8*th*

THURSDAY 10*th*   THURSDAY 9*th*

FRIDAY 11*th*   FRIDAY 10*th*

SATURDAY 12*th*   SATURDAY 11*th*

Sunday 13*th*   Sunday 12*th*

HENLEY   GEORGE WANSBROUGH

FOR fifty weeks in the year, Henley sleeps, a little placid town by the river, like its neighbours, Pangbourne and Marlow, Goring and Wallingford. At the end of June, its streets become filled with young athletes from every part of England, and from many distant countries; and the town bedecks herself as a bride for her bridegroom. At the beginning of July, the full glory of her four-days' pageant bursts on her, and the regatta begins.

After ninety years of almost unfailing repetition, Henley Regatta still retains its place as one of the festivals of the English social calendar, and ranks as the greatest of the world's regattas, whose prizes are more highly treasured than any other rowing trophies.

The coming of the motor car, which brought Henley within striking distance of London, abolished one of the greatest glories of Regatta week, the sublimated picnic of the house-boats; but how much remains! When the sun shines—and Henley is utterly dependent on the weather— what a lovely picture the Stewards' Enclosure is! Here for once man abandons his austerity of attire, and the un-numbered vivid hues of blazers rival the many-coloured glory of woman's dress.

What a feast there is, too, for the eye, in the racing, the centre and cause of all the festivity. The eight-oared rowing delights with its disciplined co-ordination, with the alter-nating fierceness and relaxation of each stroke, that makes the rhythm of its majestic progress. With the four oars there is more delicacy and touch; see with what eye-deceiving quickness the blades enter and leave the water. The pairs —how exquisitely controlled the strength that keeps that delicate craft driving forward on its true course, inclining neither to the right nor left. The scullers—what unyielding exertion there is in the single-handed struggle, what agony of exhaustion.

On Saturday of Regatta week, the final races are rowed, and the trophies presented. In the evening, with an orgy of fireworks, the Regatta comes to an end, and Henley returns to sleep for fifty weeks more.

MONDAY 14*th*   MONDAY 13*th*

TUESDAY 15*th*   TUESDAY 14*th*

WEDNESDAY 16*th*   WEDNESDAY 15*th*

THURSDAY 17*th*   THURSDAY 16*th*

FRIDAY 18*th*   FRIDAY 17*th*

SATURDAY 19*th*   SATURDAY 18*th*

𝔖𝔲𝔫𝔡𝔞𝔶 20*th*   𝔖𝔲𝔫𝔡𝔞𝔶 19*th*

LORD's is the place where, according to the old story, a
little girl once cried excitedly to her mother, "Look,
Mummy, look! There are some boys playing
cricket!". It is in fact a cricket-ground of a special character
in that on certain days of the year people go there who
hardly know a leg-break from a maiden over, just as Epsom
is the racecourse where people go who know the head of a
horse from its tail chiefly by the fact that the latter is generally
supposed to be more dangerous. This means, of course, that
Lord's is one of the national headquarters: there are cir-
cumstances in which the tribute paid by the ignorant is more
impressive than any that knowledge can pay.

But while at the Eton and Harrow, or the Oxford and
Cambridge match, ignorance is making its annual obeisance
to the game, the players "in the middle", feeling the burden
of their responsibility, are all concentrated upon their business. For it is here, while the ices and the strawberries and
cream are being eaten beyond the boundaries, that many a

famous amateur has first presented himself to the judgment of the heroes of an earlier generation who impartially decide whether the new recruit is likely to be worthy of them. First appearances at Lord's in the great matches, for one of the schools, or for one of the Universities, or for England or one of the Dominions in a Test match, are epochs in the life of the cricketer. Because of this the ignorant go to eat ices there, and because of the ignorant who go there to eat ices, this is so—a mystery the unravelling of which would throw much light on the character of the English.

It will never be unravelled. But the fact remains that to the cricketer deeds done at Lord's are sweeter than those done elsewhere. Be sure that Albert Trott, no matter how perfect the wickets in the Elysian fields, still remembers the day when he punched a ball over Lord's pavilion and that it will be an eternity before William Ward forgets his record score of 278 there which stood unequalled for one hundred and five years.

MONDAY 21*st*   MONDAY 20*th*

TUESDAY 22*nd*   TUESDAY 21*st*

WEDNESDAY 23*rd*   WEDNESDAY 22*nd*

THURSDAY 24*th*   THURSDAY 23*rd*

FRIDAY 25*th*   FRIDAY 24*th*

SATURDAY 26*th*   SATURDAY 25*th*

Sunday 27*th*   Sunday 26*th*

THE AIR PAGEANT
LORD THOMSON

ALTHOUGH the Royal Air Force first came into existence during the later stages of the World War, its solid contribution then to final victory gave it that vague but precious asset—a tradition, while the confidence now so widely felt as to its future usefulness, in peace and war, ensures for it a leading place among our national institutions.

The Hendon Air Pageant is the culmination of the R.A.F. Training Season. The units taking part have been trained at various Home Stations and represent the average standard of efficiency; hundreds of pilots are engaged, not merely star performers. Massed squadrons fly past the Royal Stand with the precision of Guardsmen on parade; others give dazzling displays of aerobatics, swoop, circle, roll, dive almost vertically, defy the laws of gravity by their speed, appear like things of life, controlled by pilots whose cool daring is equalled only by their skill. And every exercise has a purpose, a practical application to the ordinary and extraordinary duties our Air Force may be called upon to perform.

For example, a set-piece at the Pageant of 1927 was, as the event has shown, a dress rehearsal of the withdrawal of foreign residents from Kabul in British aeroplanes, and furnished a striking instance of intelligent anticipation.

No less impressive is the exhibition of the latest types of aircraft: the swaying "Helicopter" and wobbling "Pterodactyl" are signs and portents, the heralds of the next advance in man's conquest of the air.

The crowd at Hendon has a special character; nothing quite like it can be seen elsewhere. Compared to the crowds that flock to the Derby, Boat Race and Brooklands, it is more intelligent, more serious and younger, but not a whit less enthusiastic. These people are proper citizens of a mechanical age, and the Air Pageant is to them an annual rite.

Foresight, faith, courage, varied knowledge and, above all, a progressive spirit are essential for the development of aviation. These are abundantly displayed at Hendon, and this convincing proof that they exist revives and justifies calm confidence in the future of our race.

MONDAY 28*th*   MONDAY 27*th*

TUESDAY 29*th*   TUESDAY 28*th*

WEDNESDAY 30*th*   WEDNESDAY 29*th*

THURSDAY 31*st*   THURSDAY 30*th*

                               FRIDAY 31*st*

MEMORANDA

FRIDAY 1*st*

SATURDAY 2*nd*   SATURDAY 1*st*

𝕾unday 3*rd*   𝕾unday 2*nd*

COWES   GODFREY CHILDE

GOODWOOD has passed and the racing contingent
has drifted away until it shall reassemble in full
force on the Town Moor for the last of the Classics.
Scotland is taking her toll and the most conservative and
the most beautiful of the season's gatherings has begun.

There is a fitness peculiar to its association with the sea,
for she notoriously will not tolerate interference with her
ways. Thus Cowes, despite attempts made upon its ex-
clusiveness, is unique on account of its resistance towards
the unseamanlike and the parvenu. It is not snobbery, it is
conservatism—a distinction foreigners often find it difficult
to understand. True, there are moments when the younger
members, the scions one should say, of plutocracy make the
air hideous and rend the essential grace of the scene by the
noise from the exhausts of their racing motor-boats. As a
rule, however, the lawns of the R.Y.S. wear a calm unruffled
air, very much the same as the expressions upon the faces
of its principal members.

Large and clumsy-looking steam yachts lie at anchor in

the Roads, exposing their own ugliness by very contrast with the perfect grace of their sailing sisters. Miracles of white brass-burnished beauty, their tall masts gleaming in the sunlight, their proud and various burgees fluttering in the breeze—Royal Victorian, Royal Thames and many more—the Bermudian rigged eight-tonner and the two hundred ton schooner ride easily on the tides.

When the racing begins and the white sails are hauled into position the scene is transfigured: nothing can approach to the beauty of the sight. And when the wind stiffens and the ships heel before its force they are like—but what is the use? They are like themselves. When night has fallen and music comes faintly across the water, the Solent is pricked with riding lights and the white shimmering reflections of illuminated port-holes.

The grave and grey-bearded, the young seamen, all are pleasantly tired and at peace. And up above in the blue star-fretted sky, the stars are very like the mast lights. The island is vague and dim in the darkness, the town glows and twinkles from all its windows. Dinghies and pinnaces chug-chug to and from the shore with their cargoes of returning diners-out. Yes, Cowes is very English and very beautiful. Could anyone say more than that?

MONDAY 4*th*   MONDAY 3*rd*

TUESDAY 5*th*   TUESDAY 4*th*

WEDNESDAY 6*th*   WEDNESDAY 5*th*

THURSDAY 7*th*   THURSDAY 6*th*

FRIDAY 8*th*   FRIDAY 7*th*

SATURDAY 9*th*   SATURDAY 8*th*

Sunday 10*th*   Sunday 9*th*

MONDAY 11*th*   MONDAY 10*th*

TUESDAY 12*th*   TUESDAY 11*th*

WEDNESDAY 13*th*   WEDNESDAY 12*th*

THURSDAY 14*th*   THURSDAY 13*th*

FRIDAY 15*th*   FRIDAY 14*th*

SATURDAY 16*th*   SATURDAY 15*th*

Sunday 17*th*   Sunday 16*th*

URBAN SUMMER CYRIL CONNOLLY

IT has been said that everybody should attempt the "Season" once. For the unseason, or gruelling hot weather, how more than adequate the number seems! And yet, although confined to cities, how few of us possess a city sense and how little can we appreciate the aesthetic of the streets in which we dwell. Now, since travel is the subtlest form of self-expression, and the secret of travel to know the most we may expect, I have tried to indicate the quality of our urban summer lest any seeker after new experience should find the voyage suit his mood.

Waves of gusty pavement heat, the oven breath of cities, the minute and sinister yield of asphalt to the foot; all these —since heat is relative and finds nowhere else such slight attempts at mitigation—combine with the paint blisters, the buses probing through the slow twilight and sunsets streaming from the flaking posters to render London one of the great tropical cities of the world. Remember too that this London of the unseason is demotic and cosmopolitan. Study the Alexandrian flavour, the corner-houses and cafeterias, the bright mock boulevards and levantine crowds. "Neither disdain nor fear" like Sterne "to walk up a dark entry" and plunge at dusk beyond the river, where children play and women sit on doorsteps in streets that recede into a waste of suburbs and a silence broken only by the rattle of sticks on the paling or—hardly penetrating through the tin trees, brittle as the much-licked conifers in a Noah's-Ark—by lovers' voices and the grind of homing trams.

Admittedly, this adult beauty must be wrested precariously from ugliness, as a walk at Aden from the morning sun, but at least by so doing the traveller, before invalided home again, may paint his own self-portrait. "Remote, unfriended, melancholy, slow", let him afterwards look back on those golden evenings when he felt his personality lengthen with his shadow, when anonymous, and alert with fatigue, he paced the streets and peered through curtained windows, suspicious and suspected and obscure and staring —but living seasonably at last through all the urban summer and privileged to savour, as Ulysses, "les plis sinueux des vieilles capitales", and to sample as a Caliph the town's adventures, erroneous there to wander by the Bankside alleys, and forlorn through Kingsland.

MONDAY 18*th*   MONDAY 17*th*

TUESDAY 19*th*   TUESDAY 18*th*

WEDNESDAY 20*th*   WEDNESDAY 19*th*

THURSDAY 21*st*   THURSDAY 20*th*

FRIDAY 22*nd*   FRIDAY 21*st*

SATURDAY 23*rd*   SATURDAY 22*nd*

Sunday 24*th*   Sunday 23*rd*

FISHING   EDMUND BLUNDEN

WE shall never forget those early summers, when the
long twilights and music of tranquillity returned.
Fishing also returned. It was no isolated pleasure;
it was a rhythmic inevitability of the rural calendar,
a magnetism of running water or deep-built pool. There
were in the village solid labouring men, who never regarded
themselves as anglers. But on one of those soft-echoing
evenings, every year, we saw them sauntering through
pastures where mushrooms glistened, to the bream-swim.
They could not deny this annual rite. So, too, a man would
turn out *once* for cricket, a welcome votary. It was the sign
of understanding.

With the fishing season, strange events excited our small
world. No one thought of the butcher's son, likened to a
bullock, as an ingenious angler. He obviously lacked both
zeal and art. However, there he was, prowling homeward
from an unpromising shallow with a netful of those black-
tailed chub who had seemed to know everything under the
sun. He had comforted them with black-hearts. Then there

was Tardy, who beguiled roach with a little moss from the weir. But these surprises of catching hardly rivalled those of seeing. In the silver glass, some menacing eel would forage; bluish deeps revealed processions of bream, known and unknown. These moods of the fish removed them from the classification of things to catch. They were almost taboo. That pike one day which would not move a yard, though stoned, knew the law. It was not "agreed between us", when he lay isolated in that mystery.

Shall I go fishing again, except in the character of the annual worshipper, like my friend the bricklayer with his sun-hat and tricycle? Lately, I tried under the alder which always announced a perch or two beneath. My minnow swam round in patient misery; then the float dipped aside and far away into the green obscure. The perch was bright, his rosy fins and tiger-stripes made the lily dim. He had not swallowed the minnow, who hung on the line faintly gasping, while on his hook the bold-mouthed pirate eyed a worse pirate. I was no longer of the parish. I hope the minnow knew what weed would heal his tiny lip. The perch went furiously home, no doubt to be taken to-morrow by some urchin free and clever as himself. But my fishing now lies another way. When I can tell why behind that shoal of roach and dace one perch always swims with eager companionship, or what the distant thunder says to eels in fronded stones, I shall think myself an angler.

MONDAY 25*th*   MONDAY 24*th*

TUESDAY 26*th*   TUESDAY 25*th*

WEDNESDAY 27*th*   WEDNESDAY 26*th*

THURSDAY 28*th*   THURSDAY 27*th*

FRIDAY 29*th*   FRIDAY 28*th*

SATURDAY 30*th*   SATURDAY 29*th*

Sunday 31*st*   Sunday 30*th*

CRICKET   J. C. SQUIRE

AMERICANS say it is a slow game. So it is. That is one
of its charms.

I am not referring to county cricket. That is usually
slower than any other. The men are slower with their run-
making and slower getting out: and there are no compensa-
tions. The spectator, bored to inattention by a series of
maiden overs stubbornly played and a match that is bound
to end in somebody winning first-innings points, cannot
lapse into a warm reverie over the beauty of the bird-haunted
gasometer soaring into the windless blue or listen with
pleasure to the soft cooing of evening-paper sellers and men
fighting for glasses of beer in the neighbouring bar. It is
in country cricket, and especially country-house cricket, that
the tempo of cricket is to be found in its perfection.

There, on a fine day, a subdued and localised activity
merely emphasises the general prevalence of leisurely motion
and rest. The batsmen, the bowlers and the fieldsmen may
be all a-strain, but they seldom look it. Those few who at
any moment may be moving, look graceful and unhurried

to eyes watching from the pavilion verandah, from rugs on the ground or from deck chairs under the branches of bushy old elms. Even the fieldsmen, if they are placed out and are untroubled by some unseemly hurricane of fours, may be observed looking at trees, rooks, larks, flights of pigeons, absent-mindedly gazing at the pretty summer dresses in the distance, or plucking and nibbling the flowers of the field.

And the spectators are not too keen or too excited. They will grow suddenly attentive and applaud if a performer suddenly does something remarkable, and they will forget everything but the game if a dramatic finish is in sight. Otherwise they are cheerful and peaceful like turf and tree and sky: a sprinkling of idle people basking in a day stolen from the turmoil of life. This is cricket at its best—and slowest.

Village cricket is another matter: it is the game at its quickest. They may not be very good at batting: but if they can't bat they can at least get out. The village blacksmith and the village policeman are proverbial figures, subjects of many a picture in *Punch*: unlike many proverbial figures, they do actually exist. *Experte credo*: I have seen the blacksmith, in slouched cap, waistcoat, braces and dark trousers, save a match by hitting five consecutive fours to leg off good off-theory bowling.

That is cricket, too; and the most plentiful kind of cricket.

MONDAY 31*st*

MEMORANDA

MONDAY 1*st*

TUESDAY 2*nd*   TUESDAY 1*st*

WEDNESDAY 3*rd*   WEDNESDAY 2*nd*

THURSDAY 4*th*   THURSDAY 3*rd*

FRIDAY 5*th*   FRIDAY 4*th*

SATURDAY 6*th*   SATURDAY 5*th*

Sunday 7*th*   Sunday 6*th*

THE CIRCUS   SIEGFRIED SASSOON

Bobby was fishing for gudgeon in the garden pond when the housemaid called to him to come indoors at once and get ready to go to the Circus. "All right, you needn't yell", he grumbled; there was nothing to get excited about, although it was the first one he'd ever been to, for he was only eight and a half. It was an hour's drive to the town and a dusty summer afternoon. He sat at the back of the dog-cart and his mother was in front with the groom. On the barn by the wheelwright's shop there was a coloured poster of Sanger's Circus, and another on the wall behind the cabin where the wooden-legged cobbler sat fugging all day, tapping and blinking up at passers-by. Haymakers were in the fields and life seemed like a buzzing endless afternoon, humdrum and happy.

When they'd put up at the job-master's yard they waited outside on the pavement to see the Circus come along in a procession, and very soon a little phaeton bowled smoothly round the corner by the wine-merchants' windows. In it sat Lord George Sanger himself, tooling a team of six piebald ponies and raising his grey top-hat. The procession followed, slow and swaying, with wild beasts in cages, elephants with crinkly trunks and huge wrinkly trousers, and a gilded chariot with Rule Britannia reclining on the top, alone with a real live lion.

Britannia must be Lady George Sanger, thought Bobby, who believed that Lord George and his brother Lord John were the sons of a Duke and had run away from home. The performance was in the evening and if you want to know what it was like you'd better go to the Circus next time you get the chance. But what Bobby enjoyed the best was the Grand Act at the end. A lot of red-coated soldiers in white helmets charged the dervishes out in the Soudan. There was a smell of gunpowder and a great noise of shooting and shouting, and one of them got the V.C. for carrying in a wounded comrade. Going home in the dark Bobby made up his mind to fight in one of Kitchener's wars as soon as he was old enough. He didn't want to be a railway-engine driver any more.

MONDAY 8*th*   MONDAY 7*th*

TUESDAY 9*th*   TUESDAY 8*th*

WEDNESDAY 10*th*   WEDNESDAY 9*th*

THURSDAY 11*th*   THURSDAY 10*th*

FRIDAY 12*th*   FRIDAY 11*th*

SATURDAY 13*th*   SATURDAY 12*th*

Sunday 14*th*   Sunday 13*th*

MONDAY 15*th*   MONDAY 14*th*

TUESDAY 16*th*   TUESDAY 15*th*

WEDNESDAY 17*th*   WEDNESDAY 16*th*

THURSDAY 18*th*   THURSDAY 17*th*

FRIDAY 19*th*   FRIDAY 18*th*

SATURDAY 20*th*   SATURDAY 19*th*

Sunday 21*st*   Sunday 20*th*

THE HIGHLAND GATHERINGS

TYRONE GUTHRIE

Here is "The Little Ripper" from Hull; the "Emily" has brought Mr Babbit on from Stratford; "The Queen of the Mumbles" has come all the way from gallant little Wales. The glens will soon be knee-deep in orange peel and chocolate paper. Then there are small private cars—hundreds, thousands, of them—the "baby" Austins with the great big whimsey blondes from Pinner, who have come North to see if it isn't as deliciously quaint and Barrie-esque as their 'idear' of it. It is. The Tourist Bureaus have seen to that. Clear, conspicuous sign-boards direct them along admirable motor-roads past the bluest 'locks' and purplest 'mores.' Real Elders will stand outside real Kirks, real Peat-reek will rise from Shielin's; and it is a simple matter for the bureaus to arrange that groups of red-haired 'Scotties' can be overheard discussing bawbees, porridge, bluebells and whiskey in voices just like Harry Lauder's.

As to the Games themselves: socially they are no longer

a Gathering of the Clans, but of the Tribes. Cruel taxation has driven the hereditary landlords to penury in Mount Street and St Juan les Pins. And in their place come Wall Street, Lombard Street, wearing proprietary airs and Highland dress. Their Phylacteries are made broad with Tartan; Highland bonnets and Glengarry caps proclaim that their heads though bloody are unbowed.

Athletically these festivals are no longer a merely amateurish trial of strength and skill amongst the local countrymen. Energetic publicity is bringing them into line with similar events in America. Each year sees bigger, bonnier, better entries. Velvet-clad tots twirl and bounce by millions upon spring-boards—their ringlets whacking against crochet collars; pine trees are thrown about by excited policemen. The blondes from Pinner are shrill with pleasure and find it all too deliciously like an advertisement for Quaker Oats.

Let us withdraw, Reader Dear, let us turn our pince-nez resolutely to the hill-tops; high up among the heather the toot of baby cars mingles drowsily with the hum of bees. Far, far below a ribbon of dust, a procession of black thrumming dots—Pan's funeral—shows us the Games are over, the cars are moving on. As the shadows grow long, as the slow exquisite Northern twilight falls, let us muse awhile on the glory that is gone...when the fiery cross flew from glen to glen, when the Pibroch echoed among the rocks, when the Young Chevalier crossed to Skye, when Albert shot his first stag; before Scotsmen were confined to such parts of their Native Land as the blondes do not prefer; to Glasgow, Dundee, Birmingham, Belfast and Calcutta.

MONDAY 22*nd*   MONDAY 21*st*

TUESDAY 23*rd*   TUESDAY 22*nd*

WEDNESDAY 24*th*   WEDNESDAY 23*rd*

THURSDAY 25*th*   THURSDAY 24*th*

FRIDAY 26*th*   FRIDAY 25*th*

SATURDAY 27*th*   SATURDAY 26*th*

Sunday 28*th*   Sunday 27*th*

THE RIVER   H. M. TOMLINSON

FROM a ship inward bound after a long voyage, a traveller sees London River, with an early morning tide and in the right weather, as if it had been created of new and bright elements for that occasion. It might be the inauguration. With an impetuous wind and a bold sunrise the shores and the tideway appear to have a lively concern with the swift movements of the shipping. The youthful brilliance of the scene dazzles a traveller, who comes up from below to see where his ship is. Its vigour gives him the doubt that his ship's speed in that blustering fairway is too great; after the repose of the voyage, this sudden noise of rushing powers and the flaring of quick waters in an early sun makes him wonder whether the going is not a bit too fast.

If he is a stranger, he might guess that the City of London, when they moored in the midst of it, would be of new marble palaces with golden pinnacles. London River is renewed at high-water every day. The galleys became the East India-men, which turned into clippers, and the clippers became liners under motor power; and all these changes were as the flickering of shapes before the wind in the morning light, leaving no trace. There is only the latest liner in the sunrise. It is even raw, this new ship in a rude wind and a brazen light. But the traveller does not feel like that, when he is a Londoner, and his ship is bound outward down Blackwall Reach at nightfall. The shadows of the galleys are there then, memories of the frigates and the clippers. Not only Hudson and Frobisher and Cook, and the company which went down Blackwall Stairs to board the three ships in the river bound for America to begin the United States—you may still see the cobble-stones of the beginning of that journey—but the clear recollection of a day in the war years, and Scott's "Discovery" heading down stream; she hauled out from the South West India Docks.

Here the shadows are. London and its river are old. They are dark and brooding, not because the sun has just gone, but with the centuries, and great things accomplished.

MONDAY 29*th*   MONDAY 28*th*

TUESDAY 30*th*   TUESDAY 29*th*

                                       WEDNESDAY 30*th*

MEMORANDA

Autumn

"THOU gentle sprite! Whose empire is the dark green links, and whose votaries wield the bending club and speed the whizzing ball, art as dear to us now in the sere and yellow leaf as when first we flew to share in thy health-inspiring rites with the flush and ardour of boyhood."

So wrote an engaging old gentleman seventy-two years ago and I love to copy down his words. He disapproved of the "modern" game, played with irons instead of his beloved spoons. He was not a good prophet, for he thought that these interlopers were "obviously of an unchangeable character" and that the way to win a medal was "to give your iron clubs a holiday".

What would he say if he could come back to see men playing less than eighteen strokes in a whole round with wooden clubs and all the rest with "graded" irons and hybrids sprung from stumpy-headed niblicks? What would he say if he saw them taking short cuts where once had been seas of whins and slashing their way home with a drive and a chip where Allan Robertson played three short spoon shots?

Would he deem golf ruined, robbed of all subtlety, a mere matter of crude hitting, or would he think the champions of to-day demi-gods? I fear he would be unhappy but he would come, I hope, to see in time that certain things were unchanged.

There is the fun of beating your man, of seeing him delving in a bunker when you are on the green, of holing in the odd and whispering to yourself, "Now take it out of that!" There is the fun of beating the wind, either by direct frontal attack or making it a slave and an ally with the artistic slice, the cunning shade of draw. There is the fun of beating the links itself, of raising the ball from a cup or witching it away from a hanging lie, sinking down almost on to the right knee.

As long as these things remained the old gentleman would think his gentle sprite not wholly corrupted.

MEMORANDA

WEDNESDAY 1*st*

THURSDAY 2*nd*   THURSDAY 1*st*

FRIDAY 3*rd*   FRIDAY 2*nd*

SATURDAY 4*th*   SATURDAY 3*rd*

Sunday 5*th*   Sunday 4*th*

MONDAY 6*th*

MONDAY 5*th*

TUESDAY 7*th*

TUESDAY 6*th*

WEDNESDAY 8*th*

WEDNESDAY 7*th*

THURSDAY 9*th*

THURSDAY 8*th*

FRIDAY 10*th*

FRIDAY 9*th*

SATURDAY 11*th*

SATURDAY 10*th*

Sunday 12*th*

Sunday 11*th*

SHOOTING THE MARQUIS OF TWEEDDALE

HOOTING, originally merely a means of varying the diet, has come to be regarded as one of our most manly sports. It gives enormous pleasure to those who, when men were shooting one another, were busily engaged in other more important occupations and who are now able to devote their well-earned leisure to it. In fact the war profiteer has become a perfect devil among the pheasants.

It should be explained for the benefit of the uninitiated that shooting can be either "sporting" or "unsporting". It is, for instance, considered unsporting to shoot a pheasant when seated, or to shoot a bird when running unless he has been incapacitated from flying by a previous and only partially successful shot, when it is considered chivalrous to continue firing until the quarry is also unable to run. Whereas the running rabbit is deemed fair game, it is considered most unsporting to shoot the fox either sitting or running; it is however the acme of good sportsmanship to chase him until an opportunity occurs for the dogs to bite him to death.

Anyone not able to understand these subtle distinctions is un-English and outside the pale.

One of the reasons why the Bolsheviks are so *mal vus* in England is undoubtedly due to their unsporting way of destroying the superfluous population; no gentleman would shoot his social superiors without giving them a sporting chance. One cannot help comparing the Bolshevik, going round his prison selecting the quota for the next shooting, with the war profiteer going round his rearing field, and congratulating himself on the sprightliness of his future victims.

I do not suppose the bird itself cares much how it dies. It is our creed however to give the quarry what is called a "sporting chance", which means that one drives the birds high and fast with the idea that they get either killed or wounded, thus, in the latter case, giving the dogs a sporting chance.

The fact is that shooting is indefensible from a humanitarian point of view and is only enjoyable to those who ignore the feelings of the hunted. I myself have no illusions on the matter. I enjoy shooting, but I do not attempt to convince myself that the pheasant or rabbit enjoys the day's sport or takes part in it willingly. Furthermore I believe that shooting would be much less popular if the pheasant could shoot back; and I personally even take exception to sportsmen who direct occasional shots at their fellow "guns"; in fact, if this all too prevalent practice were to increase, I should adopt a less dangerous sport for my declining years.

MONDAY 13*th*   MONDAY 12*th*

TUESDAY 14*th*   TUESDAY 13*th*

WEDNESDAY 15*th*   WEDNESDAY 14*th*

THURSDAY 16*th*   THURSDAY 15*th*

FRIDAY 17*th*   FRIDAY 16*th*

SATURDAY 18*th*   SATURDAY 17*th*

Sunday 19*th*   Sunday 18*th*

WEEK-ENDS   CHRISTOPHER SCAIFE

THE week ends with a sigh and a lift of the eyelid; faces peer through window panes from Whitehall to Gracechurch Street, and towards eleven a few directors and hereditary underwriters leave their offices; by one the last slave of avarice or circumstance has quit the professional for the domestic treadmill.

The year is sinking through the land; avenues are full of silent movement, chestnuts and walnuts among the wet leaves. We must be there for tea—close the window, the draught spoils my smoke—heavy lorries make motoring funereal, we shall barely do the fifty miles within the hour. How delightful to see you; there's the woman who sings, and that Anglo-Indian bore, and the young jazz Baronet with his partner; who's the shimmering voluptuary with a sandwich? What—no—really! There will be music after dinner;—"odours when sweet violets sicken"—and then that numskull Sir will say "d'you know this one" and we shall have the Savoy band over the wire.

Breakfast at ten; does no one go to church nowadays? Anyway, not on a raw, damp, gusty day like this. Who has the energy to do anything in the morning; shall we go and pick an apple before lunch? I wish one didn't eat so much, its horrible sleeping in the afternoon; one might read, but the man who forgot his *Eno's* has taken the book I want. That sleek female *is* attractive in a sort of a way. This little parlour with the fire—one of the few possible spots in the building: do you know, before tea I had no idea that anyone could understand me half so well as you; I love the country at this time of year, a time of resting—of comfort—embrace—*you* know what I mean. A last whiskey and soda? Champagne and billiards always give me a headache;— I was in Cooch Behar in ninety-four—for ever and ever, Amen.

Mr So-and-So's car at nine, and those four catch the train at half-past; the Morris at ten-fifteen and the Daimler at eleven. Goodbye, goodbye, I hope I never see you again; what a lovely time its been. Goodbye, goodbye—thirty-five, forty, forty-five, fifty—please drive slowly through the mist. Lunch, dinner, and dinner again.

The week begins with a rush and a yawn; faces peer through window panes in Gracechurch Street and White-hall——

MONDAY 20*th*   MONDAY 19*th*

TUESDAY 21*st*   TUESDAY 20*th*

WEDNESDAY 22*nd*   WEDNESDAY 21*st*

THURSDAY 23*rd*   THURSDAY 22*nd*

FRIDAY 24*th*   FRIDAY 23*rd*

SATURDAY 25*th*   SATURDAY 24*th*

Sunday 26*th*   Sunday 25*th*

THE LORD MAYOR'S SHOW   CHRISTOPHER SYKES

WHAT a grand notion is chewing the cud. Rabelais must have rejoiced in the knowledge that one animal had seven bellies—bellies, saving that last large belly, of a fastidious rather than of a ravenous character —bellies with personality. Six times is each dish titivated by each of the gourmets—to be gorged upon by the last of this strange company—a gourmand. A man of action in the midst of men of ideas. I like him the least. I hope that you and I are not of his following, but I fear that we may be.

Our age is already devouring much that the past has merely tasted. When our grandfathers scoffed at country fairs—country fairs flourished; they were not self-conscious. Now that we consider country fairs to be rather beautiful they become tedious. What few such festivals I have attended have been marked with singular sophistication. The grave of the Lord Mayor's Show is likewise being digged.

Its tombstone will be of the Arts and Crafts Society's making....

Of how many pasts is the Show a memorial. Of how many tastes does it preserve an eccentricity. An armoured horseman bequeathed by the Middle Ages rides before a coach and coachman that are symbols of the eighteenth century. The robes are an uninterrupted attempt to convert Gothic into classical, while the procession itself is a topical version of a Roman triumph, and it is in such fantastic order that the guardians of the City go to their banquet, of whose glory a healthy age has deprived everything but the name.

Gog and Magog are not quite old enough to be thought exquisite; only allow a few years and they will be works of art—but until that melancholy period long may they wind their insane path through the City endearingly unobserved.

MONDAY 27*th*   MONDAY 26*th*

TUESDAY 28*th*   TUESDAY 27*th*

WEDNESDAY 29*th*   WEDNESDAY 28*th*

THURSDAY 30*th*   THURSDAY 29*th*

FRIDAY 31*st*   FRIDAY 30*th*

SATURDAY 31*st*

MEMORANDA

SATURDAY 1st

𝔖𝔲𝔫𝔡𝔞𝔶 2nd   𝔖𝔲𝔫𝔡𝔞𝔶 1st

A MUSICIAN on Fox-hunting! The connection between Diana the Huntress and Euterpe is not obvious. The most far-fetched analogies can however be proved. One might say that the process of musical composition is not unlike that of hunting a fox. The theme, like its vulpine counterpart, may prove a "flyer" and provide good sport, or it may turn out to be merely a "cowardly, short-running traitor, no better than a 'are". Or again, one might point to the fact that nothing can express the exhilaration of the chase more vividly than music. Consider the Ride of the Valkyries, Mozart's Hunting Quartette, passages in the Fugues and Concertos of Bach. Could Surtees or John Leech do the thing more effectively?

The Hunting-field (every Englishman should remember) is a forcing-bed for the virtues that have contributed to England's greatness. The Duke of Wellington said that Waterloo was won on the Hunting-field. The phrase has been wilfully misquoted by school-masters.

Kipling, that great authority on Empire-building, has spoken of "flannelled fools and muddied oafs". Never, as far as I am aware, has he spoken disrespectfully of Fox-hunting.

"A clear head, nice observation, quick apprehension, undaunted courage, strength of constitution", these are the qualities cited by Peter Beckford as necessary for the perfect huntsman. They are also the qualities that lead to Victory.

But the Hunting-field is not only a nursery for patriots. There are other, more amiable aspects. From the episodes of Rosa MacDermott and Lord Marchhare, of Miss de Glancey and old Lord Ladythorne of Tantivy Castle up to the latest divorce case in this morning's paper, wherever hounds, horses and ladies and gentlemen are gathered together, there Cupid also has been present, mounted on a miniature Pegasus, discharging his deadly, adorable darts.

And what beauty there is, too, in the pageantry of Fox-hunting! Who can view without a quickening of the pulses the spectacle of the pack in full cry across the countryside, the elegance of horsemanship, the vivid éclat of costume?

Beauty, excitement, courage, love; does not the Hunting-field supply all the things that men most desire?

MONDAY 3rd

MONDAY 2nd

TUESDAY 4th

TUESDAY 3rd

WEDNESDAY 5th

WEDNESDAY 4th

THURSDAY 6th

THURSDAY 5th

FRIDAY 7th

FRIDAY 6th

SATURDAY 8th

SATURDAY 7th

Sunday 9th

Sunday 8th

MONDAY 10*th*   MONDAY 9*th*

TUESDAY 11*th*   TUESDAY 10*th*

WEDNESDAY 12*th*   WEDNESDAY 11*th*

THURSDAY 13*th*   THURSDAY 12*th*

FRIDAY 14*th*   FRIDAY 13*th*

SATURDAY 15*th*   SATURDAY 14*th*

Sunday 16*th*   Sunday 15*th*

THE BALLET   RAYMOND MORTIMER

An extract from a future History

THE Muscovite dancers who had first come to London as the heralds of a degrading alliance returned as emigrants from the most glorious of revolutions. But these malecontents now sought their inspiration in the gaunt saturnalia of Deauville and the Lido, instead of in the virtuous celebrations of the *dvor* and the *mir*. The Seine had swallowed up the Volga, and the Ballet was Russian only in name. The saner school of *cognoscenti* was often heard to lament this development. But a considerable war had intervened. And while Moscow had revived painting and the drama by restoring to them their didactic obligations, the burgesses of Western Europe asserted paradoxically that Form was more significant than Content, and that Art had no purpose save herself. It is difficult for us now to comprehend how the pictures of a Braque and a Picasso, the compositions of a Prokofieff and a Stravinsky, the poems of a Cocteau and a Sitwell, could excite anything but derision. But when introduced by the

129

Russian dancers the works of these charlatans won general applause. A fickle public forgot the masterpieces of Landseer and Sullivan. The first pencils of the age could no longer find a patron. Frampton and Collier expired in indigence, Noyes and Dell sought asylum on the banks of the Potomac.

The annual visits of the Ballet are therefore occasions of painful interest to the historian. There are some still alive who can remember the transports which these entertainments provoked, performed as they were by dancers less remarkable for their agility in pantomime than for their immodest costume and ambiguous physique. The theatre was thronged with painted beauties and would-be wits, and the merits of the various jigsters were canvassed with an ardour which the economic issues of that critical period could never excite. Penurious aristocrats circulated in the *foyer* as scavengers for the vilest news-sheets, and within twelve hours the scullery-maids of Sydney learned from the ether that Lady Castlerosse had worn her cairngorms, or that the obliging Merrick had been seen in converse with the bearded historian of Elizabeth. Amid general enthusiasm the prophet of tortuous inflation bore off a *ballerina* as his bride. It was noticed, however, that the Court held aloof. The clergy made just comparisons in favour of the preceding and sterner age, while the young were accused of emulating in their manners the most degraded of the Valois.

MONDAY 17*th*   MONDAY 16*th*

TUESDAY 18*th*   TUESDAY 17*th*

WEDNESDAY 19*th*   WEDNESDAY 18*th*

THURSDAY 20*th*   THURSDAY 19*th*

FRIDAY 21*st*   FRIDAY 20*th*

SATURDAY 22*nd*   SATURDAY 21*st*

Sunday 23*rd*   Sunday 22*nd*

MONDAY 24*th*   MONDAY 23*rd*

TUESDAY 25*th*   TUESDAY 24*th*

WEDNESDAY 26*th*   WEDNESDAY 25*th*

THURSDAY 27*th*   THURSDAY 26*th*

FRIDAY 28*th*   FRIDAY 27*th*

SATURDAY 29*th*   SATURDAY 28*th*

Sunday 30*th*   Sunday 29*th*

TWICKENHAM   HUGH WALPOLE

Y OU take your place by the ropes an hour before the
game. No grand seat for *you* if you are to taste the
real savour of the drama. The crowd gathers, you
are pressed forwards, backwards; in front of you, to your
right and left the empty stands rise, gaunt, gigantic, pro-
tecting with self-confident pride that virgin field so miracu-
lously green, so brilliantly coloured.

The clock tells you that there is an hour to wait—a jerk
of the minute hand and there are only a few moments remaining: now those gaunt stands are black with people
and already the band is moving from its circle on the green,
a great cheer comes from the very heart of the soil, and
figures are running forward in patterns, perpetually forming
and breaking, as though to the rhythm of universal music.

The ball rises and at once you yourself are moving with it.
You have the *agony* of participation as surely as no other in
that crowd can have it. From the moment until the end
you are drawn out and pulled back again as the rhythm
commands you. With every scrum, as the figures cluster,

there comes that halting pause; your heart seems to cease its beating, and then the rhythm lengthens again and the most lovely sight in the world is created against that dazzling green—the ball swinging, the four figures moving in line from touch to touch. With the movement a roar makes the ground under you tremble, the rhythm breaks into notes of check and counter-check and check again, and it may be, if you are lucky, that there is that ecstatic sense of strength and triumph when the solitary figure, freed at last from every hindrance, touches earth behind the Posts; after the thunder there is a silence almost of extinction.

It has been a moment of time and through the dusk the lights of fifty thousand matches sparkle like fire-flies behind fifty thousand pipes; your soul returns to that body where for a brief space it has its habitation.

MONDAY 1*st*   MONDAY 30*th*

TUESDAY 2*nd*   TUESDAY 1*st*

WEDNESDAY 3*rd*   WEDNESDAY 2*nd*

THURSDAY 4*th*   THURSDAY 3*rd*

FRIDAY 5*th*   FRIDAY 4*th*

SATURDAY 6*th*   SATURDAY 5*th*

Sunday 7*th*   Sunday 6*th*

MONDAY 8*th*   MONDAY 7*th*

TUESDAY 9*th*   TUESDAY 8*th*

WEDNESDAY 10*th*   WEDNESDAY 9*th*

THURSDAY 11*th*   THURSDAY 10*th*

FRIDAY 12*th*   FRIDAY 11*th*

SATURDAY 13*th*   SATURDAY 12*th*

𝔖𝔲𝔫𝔡𝔞𝔶 14*th*   𝔖𝔲𝔫𝔡𝔞𝔶 13*th*

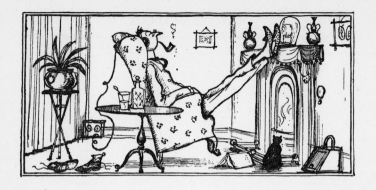

QUIET EVENINGS   JOHN VAN DRUTEN

THE day arrives when it becomes an event, that peaceful evening with a book, in one's favourite chair; when it becomes something planned in advance, like any social engagement, instead of happening naturally, all by itself, two or three times a week, which is the normal way of it. You look forward to it; you say that next Tuesday you will have a quiet evening, and you refuse all other invitations. Next Tuesday comes. It takes you a long time to set the stage, to remember which is your favourite chair, to make up the fire, and arrange the light, to answer the telephone or take off the receiver, to get into dressing-gown and slippers, and to find the pipe, long since replaced by cigarettes.

And then, there comes the problem of how the evening shall be spent. Reading is the general idea but, unless there is something momentously new, it is hard to select what you are going to read. There is, for example, that novel translated from the German, which everyone says is such a masterpiece, but even if you read steadily until three in the morning you will not get through more than the first two hundred pages, and when are you going to find the time to read the remaining five hundred?

There are letters that require answering, but so many of them that you cannot decide on which to begin. In any case, they have all waited too long. The address book is in what the Paycock called "a state of chassis", and you have promised yourself the expenditure of a couple of hours on making a new one; the gramophone records are badly in need of sorting, and so are the contents of the desk. But all these things seem such a waste of time on your one rare, quiet evening. You wander around disconsolately, turning away from this and that; in the end you probably go to bed at half-past ten.

It has been an uncomfortable experience, for it has revealed to you your own inadequacy. You must either stop having quiet evenings or have more of them. They are matters of habit; when they become isolated instances your fireside is apt to take revenge for your neglect of it.

MONDAY 15*th*   MONDAY 14*th*

TUESDAY 16*th*   TUESDAY 15*th*

WEDNESDAY 17*th*   WEDNESDAY 16*th*

THURSDAY 18*th*   THURSDAY 17*th*

FRIDAY 19*th*   FRIDAY 18*th*

SATURDAY 20*th*   SATURDAY 19*th*

Sunday 21*st*   Sunday 20*th*

1930   DECEMBER   1931

MONDAY 22nd   MONDAY 21st

TUESDAY 23rd   TUESDAY 22nd

WEDNESDAY 24th   WEDNESDAY 23rd

THURSDAY 25th   THURSDAY 24th

FRIDAY 26th   FRIDAY 25th

SATURDAY 27th   SATURDAY 26th

Sunday 28th   Sunday 27th

CHRISTMAS PRESENTS   RICHARD ELWES

THIS essay is going to be a very simple affair. It is to be constructed upon a most pregnant theme and all that is necessary is a little patient research. No cheap originality shall be allowed to mar its ordered progress. It shall just proceed according to respectable precedent and thus it will certainly be extraordinarily funny.

The ample stocks of traditional material must first be reviewed, properly tabulated in a business-like manner.

1. Tender but ill-chosen purchases for spouse by affectionate wife, e.g. ties and cigars. Comical assumption of delight on part of donee. Subsequent clandestine disposal of. (This is a good one and always was.)

2. Unwelcome presentation to penurious couple from undiscerning but affluent aunt. Prominent display of during her visit. Immediate riddance of upon her departure. Subsequent discovery by her of this disingenuous manœuvre. Collapse of "expectations". (Slightly satirical this, but funny.)

3. Accidental or jocular misdirection of parcels, e.g. warm flannel bloomers, charitably intended for Great Aunt Jane, go to irascible Colonel, or *Saucy Stories*, meant for Bertie, go to Archdeacon. (Tremendous fun.)

4. Mutual misappropriation of each other's presents by children and grown-ups, e.g. Papa engrossed in little Tommy's steam engine; little Tommy discovered vomiting with Papa's cigars. (This is rather coarse but has a moral.)

5. Studies of the more recognisable celebrities engaged in characteristic Yuletide (good!) benevolence, e.g. Mr Shaw presenting himself with a limited edition, numbered and signed, of the only decent plays ever written, or Mrs Wilhelmina Stitch giving *The Fragrant Minute* in whole vellum to Miss Gertrude Stein. (All this is very witty and topical and bound to go down.)

6. Variation on the foregoing. Development of the Barrie whimsy. He has given the proceeds of *Peter Pan* to a children's hospital. So let Mr Noel Coward assign the rights in *Fallen Angels* to an Inebriates' Home and let Dr Stopes present the doubtless unwelcome profits accruing from all her works to Queen Charlotte's Lying-in Hospital.

But stay! I see I am betrayed into forsaking the security of the well-worn path at last. This must be stopped at once. It must, to use a learned phrase, utterly cease and determine. And so must this essay. It must utterly cease before it is hardly begun. Never mind, these sprightly materials will all be invaluable for next year.

MONDAY 29*th*   MONDAY 28*th*

TUESDAY 30*th*   TUESDAY 29*th*

WEDNESDAY 31*st*   WEDNESDAY 30*th*

THURSDAY 31*st*

MEMORANDA

MEMORANDA